STUCK OUTSIDE

Andrew Taylor

STUCK OUTSIDE

The Limits of Progressive Criminal Legal System Reform in an Inequitable Society

The Carceral Studies Collection

Collection editors
Dr Ian Cummins & Dr R. Anna Hayward

LPp

First published in 2023 by Lived Places Publishing

The authors and editors have made every effort to ensure the accuracy of information contained in this publication, but assumes no responsibility for any errors, inaccuracies, inconsistencies and omissions. Likewise, every effort has been made to contact copyright holders. If any copyright material has been reproduced unwittingly and without permission the Publisher will gladly receive information enabling them to rectify any error or omission in subsequent editions.

British Library Cataloguing in Publication Data
A CIP record for this book is available from the British Library

ISBN: 9781915271785 (pbk)
ISBN: 9781915271808 (ePDF)
ISBN: 9781915271792 (ePUB)

The right of Andrew Taylor to be identified as the Author of this work has been asserted by them in accordance with the Copyright, Design and Patents Act 1988.

Cover design by Fiachra McCarthy
Book design by Rachel Trolove of Twin Trail Design
Typeset by Newgen Publishing UK

Lived Places Publishing
Long Island
New York 11789

www.livedplacespublishing.com

Abstract

This book provides an introduction and example of ways in which preexisting inequalities in society can be inadvertently reproduced through reform-oriented diversion programs or other alternatives to traditional prosecution. The book is structured around a personal chronology of the author's experiences in the criminal legal system, from his initial contact with police to the arrest that led to his diversion, through his time spent in a drug court program and ending with his reflections on changes to his life 10 years after diversion. Each section includes short summaries of relevant research that highlight racial and socioeconomic disparities, giving an overview of how some of these disparities that exist prior to engagement with the legal system may persist even in the presence of referral programs such as the one from which the author benefited.

Keywords

Criminal legal system, diversion, mass incarceration, socioeconomic disparity, police violence, substance abuse, university programs, alternatives to incarceration, criminal justice, Law Enforcement Assisted Diversion, drug court,

Contents

Disclaimer and content warning

This book contains personal anecdotes from my experiences getting arrested and participating in a diversion program, and my observations during these times, as well as from my work as a researcher for the last five years. To the extent possible, I have avoided using names or locations, or for clarity's sake, have changed names in order to protect the privacy of people I refer to, especially of those I was unable to contact while writing this book. The only exceptions to this are stories in which I cite publicly available information that reveals details about an individual, in which case I use the identifying information that corresponds to the sources cited.

This book contains explicit references to, and descriptions of, situations which may cause distress. Reader discretion is advised.

Introduction

Learning objectives

- To gain an introductory understanding of how preexisting inequalities may reproduce themselves in the criminal legal system, and particularly in some types of reform programs.
- To gain an introduction to the ways access to economic resources and/or being positioned in more privileged spaces in society can facilitate a different experience of the criminal legal system.
- To gain an introduction to how the use of alternative programs has increased in some jurisdictions for some people as well as the potential benefits associated with this change.
- To gain a very brief introduction and exposure to a number of contemporary concepts in criminology, including: the way differences in tolerance for certain behaviors may affect crime statistics, broad overviews of differences in crime and victimization rates, exposure to some variety of different diversion programs, introduction to risk responsivity and need principles in program evaluation, a more nuanced understanding behind recidivism and what those statistics may signal, among other topics.

Of the times I have been stopped by and/or arrested by the police, none were more memorable than when in 2011 at 19 years old, the apartment I lived in was raided by the sheriff's department narcotics squad, and I was arrested on multiple counts of felony possession with intent to distribute narcotics. Already not "minor" charges by most colloquial definitions, the situation was escalated by a mandatory minimum enhancement, which was triggered by living within 1,000 feet of a school bus stop and carried a two-year consecutive sentence in a medium security prison for a possession with intent charge. What is most enduring in my memory of this experience is less what happened to me and more what happened to everybody else around me as I moved through the criminal legal system. I was by no means born into a rich family with any kind of special resources to tap, but in the criminal legal system, where the vast majority of people come from the bottom deciles of income and wealth, merely having middle-class parents with college degrees set me apart as a comparatively privileged person better prepared to navigate the bureaucracy that surrounded me (Looney and Turner, 2018).

Middle-class parents who could help me navigate the system is surely no small part of why instead of going to prison, I was referred to a diversion program, where I would spend the next three years under a combination of probation and alternative court supervision. This kind of socioeconomic privilege isn't the only reason. Had I been arrested 10 years prior, I would not have had the benefit of the diversion program I was referred to (because it didn't exist yet), and instead would have been sent to a medium security prison, where I almost certainly would have been physically and sexually assaulted, and likely come out of the experience even more unstable than when I went in (Mariner, 2001; Wolff and Shi, 2009).

Having had the experience of being stopped by police multiple times prior to my arrest by the narcotics squad (and a few subsequent arrests on diversion technical violations), I've found being arrested is an experience that varies quite a bit. My reactions ranged from cocky indifference, to full-on dissociation, to loudly singing Queen songs, to crying uncontrollably at the thought of going to prison. I'm not proud of any of these situations or my reactions to them, but these are nevertheless the formative experiences that years later would set me down the path of social justice and research and lead me to write this book about privilege and disparities in the criminal legal system.

The terms "privilege", "disparities", "advantage", or "social inequality" have become so widely used in popular culture and academia in our contemporary world that they may be better suited to eliciting eye rolls and exhausted sighs than anything constructive in this context. Nevertheless, for lack of better alternatives, these are terms I will use throughout this book to refer to complicated and subtle manifestations of a very simple and seemingly widely accepted set of experiences I've had: where greater access to different resources, financial, social, educational, or otherwise, facilitated by my position in society based on my race and my parents' income and education, ultimately leads to a different experience of the criminal legal system when I was faced with the potential of incarceration in prison.

Don't misinterpret my referring to these as privileges as a lack of appreciation for these outcomes. In a lot of ways, and in my opinion, what happened to me, that is a referral to diversion over prison, is what ought to happen to a lot more people who find themselves in the same situations I did. It is not what happened to many people in the same situation over decades, and it still doesn't happen in many conservative parts of the United States.

The program that I was connected with began in the late 1990s, approximately 10 years before I would be forwarded to it, so if I were a decade older, there's a good chance I would've gone to prison precisely because no alternative would have existed. Despite my gratitude for this, it is nevertheless remarkable to me the ways in which privileges I've had in my life repeatedly shifted me from punitive responses to rehabilitative ones that ultimately kept me out of jail years later.

Of the 30 or so people who entered the diversion program at the same time as me, at least a third were either terminated from the program and went to prison, or else died during the program or shortly after completing it. If I could find comparable numbers for people who instead of being diverted went directly to prison, I suspect the outcomes would be even worse. Even fewer than the people who finished the program, are the people who finished and ended up where I am now 10 years later: with a tertiary degree, or with a job at all, let alone doing something as esoteric as applied research on criminal legal system reform for local governments around the United States.

There are many different aspects of the privilege that prevented me from going to prison, while other folks who exhibited nearly identical behavior would have. For one, I was eligible for this program because, one year prior, I had been arrested on a felony drug possession charge on a college campus that operated a Law Enforcement Assisted Diversion (LEAD)-style program. This, in effect, meant that rather than being booked into jail with a record, I was taken directly to treatment, and thus, I could not be disqualified for future programs on the basis of a criminal history. I'm not aware when that college began operating that program, but it's difficult to imagine that it could have been any sooner than the 1990s. In contrast, my friend and codefendant arrested at the same time as me went to prison and was held on bail, in part, because he had a previous charge for relatively similar circumstances as mine, but without a prior LEAD-related arrest.

Furthermore, my codefendant went through a drug assessment screening that did not indicate he had a substance use disorder or dependency disorder, where I clearly did. It is a strange irony then, that I was eligible for an alternative form of punishment because of my substance-abuse problems, while this alternative would not have existed for someone in a very similar situation. Yet we exhibited similar behavior, and it's impossible for me to imagine that prison was somehow a more deserving fit for him than all of the treatment I received that wasn't strictly substance-abuse related. A vast part of my program consisted of trauma therapy, cognitive behavioral therapy designed to increase less harmful coping mechanisms, and of job and educational placement services. Why on earth society would be better by sending my codefendant to prison because he didn't have a substance use disorder, when he clearly could have benefited from at least some of these services as well, seems entirely unjustifiable.

Greater access to financial resources didn't mean simply a wholesale write off of my arrest, but instead manifested itself in access to different resources that elicited different treatment. For example, it was remarkably clear from the moment my private attorney stepped into the courtroom, that private defense made it easier, at least for me, to be connected to treatment in lieu of incarceration. In fact, to quote one of the intake counselors in the diversion program in which I'd been accepted:

> A lot of it is about respect, and there's a good chance the moment they saw that he [my private attorney] was representing you, they trusted his suggestion and that's why you're here today.
>
> (Anonymous, 2011b)

This is just one example of how it is that privileges that exist prior to any interaction with the criminal justice system continue to reproduce themselves, even among progressive approaches and changes. This book will show my reflections on that based on my personal experiences and what I know of the academic literature and other publicly available reports and data that supplements this description. Beyond that, I believe following the decade of progressive criminal justice reform that took root in states and cities across America, that we as students or practitioners, or as people involved in movement building or as anybody with an interest in this topic, owe it to ourselves and the people we serve to reconsider the ways investments in addressing larger structural inequalities can be effective in reforming the criminal legal system.

This is an interesting moment for criminal legal system reform in America. On the one hand, the past few years have seen some of the strongest calls by abolitionists for a divest and invest approach that expands beyond reforming punishment to an expansive investment in communities that will likely do more to prevent crime in the first place. On the other hand, fearmongering around crime has risen alongside a very real increase in violent crime in many places across America, creating a nascent anxiety among some that progressive changes gained in the last decades will backslide. Many people far more informed than me have continued to make arguments for why it is that divestment from the criminal legal system and investment into community may create both a more equitable criminal legal system and improve community safety. In fact, it's a core theme of the policy platform released by the Movement for Black Lives, whose demands related to tax code restructuring I personally suspect may do more to reduce disparities in the criminal legal system than any progressive criminal legal reform can do alone (Movement for Black Lives, 2016b). It is my hope with this book to add my own contribution about the limits of progressive reforms in addressing disparities, to inspire others to further study, and to advocate for investment in other aspects of society to improve safety and justice.

With all the above in mind, allow me to give you the context that led up to my arrest by the narcotics squad, and to explain how that would set the stage for my enrollment in a diversion program in lieu of prison.

Possession with intent

In 2010, at age 18, I started college. Rather than having any real interest in education, I was primarily obsessed with the idea of trying to make the 'most of my life,' a phrase as meaningless to me now as it was then. Armed with a cynical view of society and my future, I manifested this goal by engaging in as much hedonistic activity as I could possibly afford on student loans and my delicate mental health could withstand. Riding on mediocre childhood trauma, I spent a large portion of my teenage years engaging in slowly escalating drug and alcohol use. By the time I reached young adulthood at 18, my interactions with police and the criminal legal system were about to take a severe and very predictable turn. The phrase, "very predictable" is warranted here because research on childhood trauma (or "adverse childhood experiences") and its relationship to substance abuse, is just that: very predictable.[1] In fact, nowhere is that clearer than for youth detained in the criminal legal system (Baglivio et al., 2014).

Years of progressive drug use and untreated depression culminated in my seeking mental health support on a college campus, where I confided in a counselor that I was having suicidal thoughts and felt like I couldn't control my actions. After a painful but supportive hour of counseling in the student mental health center, I was released to my dorm, where I proceeded to sleep for something close to 14 hours. Failing to respond to what I suspect in hindsight were mandatory checkup calls, as I'm sure I'd passed some sort of test for high risk, police were dispatched to my dorm to verify I was safe. While it was clear I was safe, my dorm apartment was littered with opioid and other drug refuse and paraphernalia. I was immediately reported to the student housing services, who then had me taken into a Law Enforcement Assisted Diversion program (LEAD) that in lieu of traditional arrest took me on a tour of emergency rooms and treatment centers. In other words, having been found in possession of felony narcotics and drug paraphernalia was treated with what we might consider to be disciplinary action as opposed to formal arrest.

After my first stop at the emergency room had me placed immediately on an antidepressant medication (while a self-described recovering crack addict explained Jesus to me for 30 minutes), I was then whisked away to an inpatient facility, where I sat in what looked like an old family living room for what felt like hours but could have easily been 30 minutes. During this time, I gradually regained both composure and defensiveness, and thus, when I eventually met with some kind of intake counselor, who offered a blunt proposition, I was well equipped to deny him.

Specifically, the counselor said to me:

> Based on your pattern of drug use for your age, you're not eligible for inpatient treatment [*which at the time was vastly over capacity as the opioid epidemic began to surge and the young people of this city switched from meth and/or oxycontin to heroin: author's comment*]. However, you can change your answers [*i.e., lie: author's comment*] and I think we can get you in here. Because, I have to tell you, Andrew, in all my years of doing this, I've seen this happen time and time again, where if you don't come in now, I'll almost certainly see you when you're really eligible in a year or two from now, either because you've been arrested or because you've overdosed. So why don't you save yourself the pain and we can get you in now?
>
> (Anonymous, 2010b)[2]

Invigorated by my regained defensiveness as the consequences of my actions to seek treatment were starting to materialize with the reality of the shame I would feel talking to my parents, leaving school, and living in an inpatient treatment, I did what I think anyone, except people much more courageous than me, would do: I ignored his advice completely and rudely told him to fuck off and then stopped talking.

After that, I was taken to a public detox facility, where I spent about two or three hours in a waiting room that looked like a cordoned off school supply closet, while an aspiring alt rock musician explained to me how much better it was to shoot, instead of snort, ketamine, and a drunk Iraq veteran repeatedly tried to fight the intake staff while shouting homophobic slurs and calling us (me and the alt rock guy) tweakers (people who use crystal meth). I was released the next morning with a meth-addicted homeless man, who explained to me why we needed to leave this town forever and go to Las Vegas ("people will just understand us there, man"), to find my shocked and horrified parents, who I greeted full of shame, but still thoroughly walled off with defensiveness and denial.

What followed over the next year and a half was sadly predicted by the intake counselor. I dropped out of college and moved back into my mom's home where my substance abuse continued to progress. Part of the conditions of the LEAD program as opposed to arrest, was that I would complete treatment. Otherwise, there was an implication that the incident recorded by the police would be reported and charged. Thus, I began an outpatient treatment program in my hometown, where my fellow participants consisted mostly of alcoholic dads (weekend dads mostly but some full-time ones), burned-out hippies, and a handful of opioid users in their late teens and twenties. I went through the motions of treatment, ignoring my required fees and urine analysis tests (UAs), until it became clear to me that the

LEAD program requirement to enroll in treatment was not going to be enforced, and then I simply stopped going.

Not long after that a friend was hospitalized for an overdose and nearly died—not an uncommon outcome among people who used drugs, and especially during that period in Washington state, where for a variety of reasons, per capita overdose was about 25% higher than the national average.[3] With renewed anxiety for her and myself, I returned to treatment for two more weeks, before a vicious argument with my mom led me to leave her home and move into my dad's empty foreclosed house.

Living in an empty foreclosed house might sound like a particularly bleak moment to some of you, but those of you who were of age between 2008 and 2012 might remember just how common foreclosures in America were at that time. For those who don't know or don't remember, between 2008 and 2012, 11.75 million houses, representing about 2 out of 100 of all American housing units, were foreclosed on (ATTOM, 2022). To put memories to statistics, I remember the day I moved my bag of belongings from my mom's Rambler to my father's empty foreclosed house, located in what was, at the time, still a middle-class subdevelopment that four years prior had been full of new families moving in. When I moved there in 2011, of the roughly ten houses on our block, at least four were empty, and at least two of them were under foreclosure or had been subjected to short sales as a result of the recession.

From there, increasingly broke and reliant on my parents' ever declining patience and desire to support me financially, I set out to try and find some kind of employment. I tried all five of the fast-food restaurants in the part of town I could get to by bus, three retail outlets, and eventually a job fair for a hardware store. You might recall that this was a tough time to find a job. Employment losses from 2008 had not yet come back, especially not in smaller towns like mine, so it was not a great time to be looking for a job as an angsty teenager with visible substance-abuse problems and poor social skills. To exemplify just how disheartening this was, I remember showing up to a job fair for a hardware store and being one of two hundred people applying for fewer than ten entry-level retail positions. A grim time for somebody without a lot to offer. And while I wish I could say this lit a fire under me to apply for every open position and work as hard as I could, the reality is that this led to resentment, depression, anxiety, and constant self-sabotage that only stifled the job search more.

Eventually I borrowed money from my dad to enroll in a six-week nursing assistant training program with the promise of almost guaranteed job placement upon completion. And so, after six weeks, angry, bitter, depressed, and most importantly extremely broke, I got a just above minimum wage job working nights in a memory care hospice facility in a rural part of the county to which I commuted by bus for the better part of six months. To this day, that is the hardest job I have ever had, where nearly every day was filled with residents dying, nearly dying, or needing serious and intensive help toileting and grooming. For that, we made a grand total of $1.50 over minimum wage, while a friend of mine, who worked as a dishwasher at a bar about a half mile from there, made $2.00 over the minimum wage. While I really admire most of the folks I worked with at the facility, it became quite clear to me after a few months that I was not cut out for healthcare, considering I regularly gagged at the sight of human blood and feces. So continuing to try to live out the memory of advice I'd heard in the treatment program that told me to just get a job, I decided this would not be the job that turned things around for me and I was going to need a new plan.

Thus, about five months into my work as a night shift nurse's aide, still feeling lost and desperate, and with no desire to continue this newfound career track, I reenrolled in a different local university with the hope of finding a path to a more fulfilling or at least better paying career. The bank was officially confiscating my dad's house that fall and my mom and I were not speaking. I quit my job as a nurse's aide when I couldn't figure out how to coordinate the night shift, class, and bus schedules. I tried to find a room via want ads and asking among other people I knew, but unsurprisingly most of my friends were not in much better positions than me, and my social skills among strangers looking for roommates left more than a bit to be desired. As it got closer to the mandatory move date, lacking any other options, I moved in with a friend who sold drugs. He lived in an apartment and was willing to let me share his room to save money.

I wouldn't call him a successful drug dealer, or use any other euphemism for making more than minimum wage, but it's undeniable that he sold drugs, and a lot of them to twentysomethings and college students connected through me and another roommate. I wasn't completely naive and was aware that moving in meant taking on some serious risk. And to assuage my anxiety, my friend assured me that if something ever went down, he would take the fall and that should be OK. Content with this assurance, not to mention needing a place to live quickly and having alienated or distanced myself from anyone else who might've rented me a room instead, I moved in and was happy to help him find new customers in what I hoped would be a clean slate of new college friends.

Unfortunately, one customer was a second-year college student with a very serious stimulant addiction who had recently started injecting. One fall night, after missing a vein, a massive abscess formed on his arm and his roommate called the police seeking help, fearing that his roommate was overdosing. As I would learn years later from the police report, after the police arrived, he was interrogated about where his friend had got access to drugs and paraphernalia, and when questioned, told them the location of our apartment.

***

If you live an interesting enough existence, you might find, like I have, that there are some moments in your life that seemingly no amount of time, retelling, exaggerating, alcohol, or self-deprecating comedic distance can ever really reduce the strength of the memory. I remember this night very clearly if only out of the sheer absurdity of it.

I was sitting on our gross used college-kid couch, eating frozen Tater Tots, while a friend's girlfriend was roasting pumpkin seeds we had used for carving jack-o'-lanterns earlier that day (hardened criminals that we were). My friend who sold drugs was in the shower, while his supplier was playing the free-to-play online video game RuneScape on our kitchen table, and two other friends were smoking weed with our roommate in her room. Not a great scene, but pretty innocent, and not so different from average early twenties experiences, or so I'm told anyway.

Earlier that day, a friend from the apartment complex had come by to tell my friend to move all the drugs out of the house. This advice didn't come from nowhere. That friend, a Black man in his mid-thirties, who used to sell drugs, was anxious that the amount of drugs we were holding inside the apartment would be enough for a serious charge. With this advice, he tried to make the case that we would be better off storing things in a separate location. A reasonable piece of advice, but we were more afraid of being robbed than of being arrested and mostly laughed off the suggestion. Nevertheless, we eventually relented, and my roommate began packing everything into a few backpacks to take everything to another location.

Our overconfidence at the threat of arrest didn't come from nowhere, and in fact was a pretty realistic assessment of most of our, or at least my interactions, with police so far. Prior to this point, none of the at least five times I had been harassed by or stopped by the police, with drugs or while on drugs, had resulted in an actual arrest, and thus, this arrogance of our ability to continue to fly under the radar because of who we were (a.k.a. White people) was not unfounded.

In fact, this assessment didn't seem particularly unique to just the White people in this apartment. When I first began college, prior to my first arrest that had led to the LEAD program, I had met multiple other White teenage boys who either sold drugs or were in a similar "scene". One of whom, I remember very clearly, was from the Baltimore suburbs where my dad was born and lived before college took him to the West Coast in the late 1970s. He told me a story once about how he and a friend had been stopped by the police for speeding once with thousands of dollars' worth of narcotics in their parent's car.

> Thank god we weren't Black; that's all I can say.
>
> (Anonymous, 2010a)

Those were his exact words. To his credit, that's a realistic assessment of the situation. We will elaborate on this more in the next chapter, but there is no shortage of research suggesting that Black drivers are more likely to be stopped and searched than White drivers, despite small to no tangible differences in the likelihood of the recovery of contraband (particularly related to drugs), and evidence that this difference shrinks when officers are unable to ascertain the drivers race, suggesting a pretty clear racial bias (Pierson et al., 2020).

Returning to the story: as I flipped through my college course reading on the couch, ignoring the group of other teenagers around me while eating my Tater Tots, at the start of a dark, heavy rainy night, the kind you get in the early fall in the Northwest— suddenly—

Cop knock[4]

"Sheriff's department."

The door flung open, five maybe six sheriff's department members in body armor with guns drawn entered and ordered us down to the ground. They cuffed me and had me down almost immediately. They grabbed my friend out of the shower and our sobbing roommate out of her room. They gathered everyone else in the entryway of the hall and ordered anyone who wasn't a resident to leave while they began to open and tip over every drawer in the house in search of contraband. They dumped the contents of kitchen and bedroom drawers onto the floor, until eventually they found several bags of narcotics neatly arranged in the backpack we were preparing to move to another location.

As they pulled my friend, naked and shocked, out of the shower and dragged him into the living room, I'll never forget that despite all of this, he kept true to our arrangement and said:

> I'm going to speak to my lawyer, but they had nothing
> to do with this.

In contrast to his statement, what follows for me is one of the most shameful moments of my life. After gathering the three of us in the entryway of our house, the detective—a young guy not more than five or six years older than us in his mid to late twenties—said that if the two us cooperated they might not have to take us to jail, and would just take our friend, who had already confessed to being the one who actually sold drugs. Shaken by the experience and terrified of jail, my roommate and I cooperated, which is probably one of the greatest mistakes I have made in my life. In fact, if you have ever been close to this way of life, or met a lawyer, or indeed just been a person in the world paying attention to anything, someone has probably told you something like "Don't talk to the police. Wait for your lawyer". If not, let me be the first to tell you how important that advice is.

Instead of waiting for a lawyer, we agreed to talk, and they took me and my roommate into separate rooms in the apartment to interrogate us. Seconds into confessing that I was aware of my friend's operation, I thought (ignorantly) that I had fulfilled my side of the bargain to him, and I thought, by helping the police,

I was guaranteeing that I wouldn't go to jail (that's what they said would happen after all). It became clear this was a (sadly successful and predictable) ploy to get more information out of us and there was no way I wasn't going to jail. In less than five minutes, I'd incriminated myself (unbeknownst to me) and was back in the living room awaiting the ride to lockup.

If you've ever experienced a moment of feeling so overwhelmed by the shock that your body and mind seem to go straight past sadness or fear and headlong into defense mechanisms and compensation, you might understand what happened next. As they led us out of the apartment, cuffed, me in my half sweatpants without my corrective glasses, my friend now in gym shorts and nothing else, and our roommate sobbing, a huge shift came over me, and somehow, I went from despondent to elated. I don't know why or how, but somehow, I became obsessed with trying to lighten the mood. After they put us in the booking tank, I tried my best to coordinate the drunks into choruses of *Bohemian Rhapsody*, in between "your mom" jokes to my friend, clinging to some idea that somehow at least things couldn't get worse. I have no idea how this happened, and indeed in the coming years when I would go back to jail three more times, I tried and failed repeatedly to summon this elation when I felt only despair, but for some reason in that moment I felt OK.

So OK in fact, that as we waited for processing in the booking tank, I barely even registered that the same person who had almost overdosed and inadvertently been reported by his roommate got booked in with us. I clocked him half an hour after they brought us in, and only because he began to wail about being suicidal, at which point a guard came by to ask if everything was OK. I consequently learned a valuable lesson about never reporting anyone for suicidal thoughts out of fear of them being put into isolation. Coincidentally, also in the booking tank, was a friend from high school who had developed a heroin addiction and was there as he was about to be terminated from the very same diversion program I would soon enroll in. Unbeknownst to me at the time, another friend from the same school year as me, who had grown up in foster care, had been released a few days prior and was starting the same program after having been released a few days prior, though he would around two months from the time I was arrested on a relapse-related overdose. As I've already mentioned, this was a small town.

I was released on recognizance (ROR) the next morning. My previous arrest didn't appear in a background check given the LEAD-style program at the university, and as a first-time offender (on paper anyway), they let me go on ROR in less than 24 hours. In contrast, the prior arrest of my friend on a minor possession charge some years earlier showed up in the background check and a $10,000 bond was set, high enough for him to remain in jail for another month until he could find a volunteer to post bail.

The use of a financial bond at this time represented something near a 20-year high in the use of financial conditions when releasing felony defendants pretrial. From 1990 to 2009 the use imposition of any financial bail conditions for all felony defendants in large urban counties released pretrial increased from just under 40% in 1990 of all releases to 60% in 2009. This change was driven almost entirely by the expansion of private bail bond industries, estimated as at least a $14 billion industry in 2016 (Color of Change, ACLU Campaign for Smart Justice,

2017). In 1990, 65% of those released on financial bonds were using commercial bonds, rising to 80% by 2009 (Liu, Nunn and Shambaugh,2018). Of course this wasn't an urban area, but it doesn't seem unlikely that the same trends would have applied here.

That a $10,000 bond or $1,000 commercial bond could be enough to keep my friend in jail may seem hard to grasp by some, but it's an experience shared by millions of people who have bond set every day. Indeed, a Bureau of Justice Statistics (BJS) study of people detained pretrial from 1990 to 2004 suggests that five out of six people detained until disposition were there because they had a bond set that they could not afford, where only one out of six people were detained without bond, usually indicating that they were being held on a much more serious and violent crime (Cohen and Reaves, 2007). Unsurprisingly, if you review the annual incomes of those who actually go to jail, in at least one report from the Hamilton Project, the median pretrial arrest income for people held in bail was $16,000 a year in 2016, relative to $33,000 for non-incarcerated counterparts (Liu, Nunn and Shambaugh, 2018). To extrapolate on other potential financial resources for those arrested, the 2016 Survey of Consumer Finances reports that the median value of financial and total assets for households in the bottom-income quintile was $1,100, while that in the middle-income quintile (a.k.a. my parents) was close to $20,000 (Federal Reserve System, 2016). That a household with less than barely $1,000 in financial assets would find it more difficult to spend $1,000 on a bond than a household with 20 times those assets is hardly a challenging concept to grasp.

The contrast becomes even clearer when my own situation is compared to my codefendant: I had parents with some assets who could help me, my friend did not, or perhaps more importantly, I had parents who would use their assets to help me. My friend, though born with similar privilege, was even more estranged from it, so even had we both been given bail, our experiences would have been different.

Zooming out, let's unpack further why my friend had bond set in the first place while I did not. Considering we were all charged with selling narcotics and leasing an apartment to do so, the idea that prosecutors believed him when he said "we had nothing to do with it" and only my friend was guilty is not credible. If that had been the case, you might wonder why on earth they went forward with the charges against the rest of us. Another contributing factor might have been that my friend had a prior arrest and incarceration record for simple possession of a felony narcotic that had led to about two weeks in a county jail.

The significance of prior arrests or convictions as a factor in predicting compliance with pretrial release is admittedly intuitive in some respects even if it isn't always supported by research. Such a practice has a long history of study in America. Going as far back as the early 1960s with the Vera Institutes Manhattan Bail Project, there has long been an attempt to systematically determine criteria other than cash that could be used to assess who is at risk of not returning to court if released pretrial (New York (City), City Magistrates' Court, 1962). While the methods used in contemporary pretrial risk assessments (at least in New York City) have become far more advanced and account for less racial bias than early attempts, even the most advanced assessments active as of June 2020 rely on some of the same factors that apparently differentiated my friend and me, such as whether the defendant has a prior warrant or arrest or convictions or strong personal, family, and financial ties to the community (Luminosity, University of Chicago Crime Lab New York, 2020).

To an impartial observer then, that I was released on ROR while my friend was detained on bond might seem easily explainable: the risk factors were clearly different. He had a documented arrest in the last year, I did not. Yet these present a misleading characterization of the events and the ways in which social privilege facilitates their construction. I had been arrested the previous year, but it was on college campus and not documented. In terms of actual behavior, this first arrest resulting in a jail booking was my fifth interaction with a police officer in which, in any of the cases, I could have easily been arrested on drug-related charges but had been let off unsearched with warnings or diverted to alternative programs. My friend's and my prior arrests could have been for almost identical charges—in both instances we were found to be in possession of small amounts of felony narcotics (more severe in the situation that sent me to a LEAD program)—but different reactions by law enforcement facilitated by progressive reforms in one institution frequented by more privileged people reverberated to vastly different consequences a year later.

***

I left jail midmorning the following day, and took the bus back to my apartment to find it destroyed. Apparently after emptying every drawer while searching the apartment with us in it, the sheriff's department had wrecked every surface they came across to look for contraband, and everything of value, including my roommate's jewelry, laptops, various musical instruments, and a wristwatch I'd inherited from my now dead grandfather, was missing. My parents reconnected with me to help me get legal representation, and that morning they and a good friend of mine helped me to sift through the wreckage of our former apartment to find what I could take to a family friend's basement that would become my home for the next 18 months.

Meanwhile, our roommate whose parents had a lot more money than mine went back to her home in another state and immediately began a private rehab program. It's hard to enumerate empirically, but that she was not only released on ROR, but allowed to leave the state for this program and start the court ordered treatment with a head start, is not perhaps an unusual course of action for most people in our privileged situation. Considering that at this time the cost of private substance-abuse treatment in the USA may have been between $3,000 and $10,000 for an intensive outpatient treatment program in 2021 dollars, that there is a clear bias to allow out of state travel and shorter required supervision periods to those able to afford private treatment is highly intuitive.[5]

The lawyer my parents connected me to was a fascinating guy. He was a private defense attorney and former FBI investigator, who operated out of a fancy office in a nice part of town. Perhaps to name a bizarre coincidence, he told me that he knew a detective who was part of the narcotics squad that arrested us from his involvement in a domestic violence case. Out of a sort of perverse curiosity and hoping for a villainous answer I asked what him what the detective was like, and he gave me what I thought was an oddly sympathetic answer:

> He was a really great Iraq veteran, and you know those guys come back and they just can't see they're not at war anymore.
>
> (Anonymous, 2011a)

Disappointed by not getting the cartoonish depiction of the cop I was hoping, I dropped it after that. I did, however, continue to call and ask the lawyer if there was anything we could do about all the missing valuables from our apartment; I was becoming minorly obsessed with the watch I'd inherited from my grandfather. Eventually this seemed to wear on him, and he gave me this blunt answer:

> Nothing was reported to the evidence room for asset forfeiture, but look, this happens all the time and it wouldn't surprise me if things were just gone. What you need to understand is that to these guys, for them to do their job, you're not a person, and they just can't see you that way.
>
> (Anonymous, 2011a)

As an aside: about two years later as part of my diversion programming I would be required to write a letter to my arresting officer thanking him for arresting me and thus "facilitating" my entry into the diversion programming. It took me 15 tries to write a letter with a sufficient lack of sarcasm and cursing to be accepted.

Regardless, now armed with private legal defense, within a few weeks of being released, despite being initially banned from returning to college, I met with my political economy professor who had the following two things to say to me:

> All drugs should be legalized and these charges brought against you are unjustifiable. You will finish the course entirely off campus if need be.
>
> (Anonymous, 2011c)

> Everything that's wrong and hard about your experience now, imagine what it would be like if you were Black, or if you were Black in Baltimore.
>
> (Anonymous, 2011c)

Thanks in part to his testimonial on my behalf, I was allowed to remain enrolled in college and receive credit for that quarter's coursework. This meant that by the time I would start the diversion program a few months later, I would start from a position of already being in compliance with program requirements, which made it considerably easier to avoid termination from the program and to reap the benefits of therapy with only brief returns to jail and never being sent to prison. As will be elaborated on in chapter 2, this is a position of privilege that most people do not start with, and that for those unable to locate a job or enroll in a college program will ultimately lead to their termination from the program and sentencing to prison. And so on I went to the diversion program, still enrolled in college, while my roommate awaited sentencing to prison in jail.

***

This story shows many clear instances in which preexisting resources (in this case, private legal defense and college enrollment) or privilege facilitated access most often lead to a different outcome in the criminal legal system. The rest of this book will elaborate on this point in greater detail.

Chapter 1 will provide more anecdotes from my life and the lives of people around me that relate to differences in treatment by police or other criminal legal actors as people enter the criminal legal system—at times reflecting brazenly different treatment for identical behavior and also detailing ways in which the justification based on different behavior may be largely mediated by place and privilege. I will summarize some of the literature that exists on differential treatment in police behavior as well as the difference between law enforcement responses to similar behavior, in general, among high-risk populations targeted in "focused deterrence strategies", and how university campus security programs approach similar behavior.

Chapter 2 will elaborate on my experience within the diversion program I was referred to and the ways in which privilege facilitated easier compliance with the requirements, thereby providing a greater likelihood of "successful" discharge from the program and a path to positive and prosocial changes in my life. Additionally, I will contrast this with experiences of people deemed ineligible for diversion programs, and compare this with the literature on "what works" in terms of facilitating positive social change in the lives of people arrested with a critical eye to what extent this may reflect a reproduction of existing privilege.

Finally, chapter 3 will contrast the experiences of my life now, 10 years later as I write this, with the experiences of others I know who were referred to the same program around the same time. Not all of us "made it" by which I mean that a decent number of people who started the program died, went to prison, or are still injecting drugs or drinking themselves to death. Often, though of course not always, a critical factor seems to be how much social privilege we had when we started the program. I hope that my memories of my fellow participants and my grasp of some of the literature and other data that exists can help to further our understanding of how disparities reproduce themselves throughout the criminal legal system, with the ultimate goal of stimulating new and better ideas for how best to address these.

1
Entering

Learning objectives

- To understand the extent to which differences in law enforcement "tolerance" may influence who is arrested, and subsequently incarcerated, and what this means from the continuum of arrest to rearrest after release.
- To understand a few specific examples of where tolerance is clearly uneven, through comparisons of focused deterrence strategies to elite university policy for young adults of roughly the same age range.
- To obtain some exposure to tertiary risk of police violence from increased police contact.
- To understand that where to focus police resources is a complicated question, in part facilitated by stark disparities in neighborhood violence, self-reported crime victimization, and exposure to police violence or excessively punitive contact.

My first memory of being stopped by the police is from when I was 14 years old. It was evening on a cold, mostly empty, small-town Pacific Northwest street. A friend and I were waiting for the bus to take us back to where my mom lived in an unincorporated portion of a small county in Washington state. This was not a large town (at this point it was mostly trees and strip malls plus a five-block "downtown"), and everything, including the buses, tended to shut down not long into Sunday night. Said friend and I had spent Sunday engaged in such high-quality extracurricular activities as trying and failing to shoplift Silly String from a strip mall dollar store and throwing gummy candy at the handful of cars driving past.

At one point, we hit a car with the aforementioned candy and heard a much louder than expected:

Dent like a rock hitting a tin wall

At which point, being honest and honorable people, we immediately sprinted as fast as we could to the next bus stop, out of fear they would notice us, or worse, yell at us.

Now if you've ever tried to catch a bus in a small town or rural area or basically anywhere other than in a major city in America on a Sunday, then you know that if the bus comes at all (or even exists), it comes somewhere between every 30 minutes and every 3 hours. Consequently you'll spend a lot of time waiting for the bus. This meant that after making our escape from the driver whose car we may or may not have damaged, we had plenty of time to do anything else, such as start pushing leftover shopping carts at each other trying to see how loud of crashing sound we could make.

I'd say after at least the third or fourth shopping cart relayed a sound of

crash of metal on metal,

four cop cars sped around the corner, hit their lights, pulled up through the two parking lot entrances, and surrounded us at the bus stop.

Astonished, we froze in place while the police yelled for us to put our hands up. Two cops ordered my friend to walk backward slowly while they prepared to search him. Meanwhile, one older cop proceeded to ask me if I'd been hurt and if I was all right to speak. Completely stunned and now wondering what possible laws—

> did they know about the dollar store Silly String somehow? Is it illegal to have shopping carts away from the store because we didn't move them there?)

—I could've broken by pushing an abandoned shopping cart were, I responded monosyllabically.

"Yes, of course I'm fine."

"Is the bus still coming?"

"What's going on?"

The cop, becoming increasingly annoyed and relieved at the same time, eventually radioed something, then proceeded to apologize to me. Apparently, they received a call that someone was being held hostage at a bus stop, and the description of the victim matched me and that of the perpetrator my friend. Whether to reassure me or out of sheer frustration, the cop went on to explain to me that after 9/11, they'd been getting a lot of fake tip-offs like this, and apparently this was making his job harder. Go figure, poor him.

Meanwhile, not 15 feet away, two other cops were patting down and searching my friend.

"You mind telling us why someone with your exact description was reported to be holding someone hostage at a bus stop with a knife?"

"What?"

"So you don't know anything about a knife? Is this your friend here?"

When the cops failed to find a knife and after it was revealed that I was in fact, not being held hostage, the cop speaking to me gave one more apology and then all four cars left.

My friend and I didn't talk about this for a long time, except sometimes as a story we would tell to elicit almost guaranteed shock value laughs at parties for the next several years. For years, I could never understand how the police could have made that mistake, and while I mostly laughed about this as a teenager, as I got older I came to feel very lucky this worked out as safely as it did.

To be honest to this day I still have no idea why or how this happened. For years I was content to just have no idea, as after all everything worked out fine for us. This changed for me (revealing of my ignorance as it might be to admit) after being arrested by the narcotics squad and as I became more and more aware of racial bias in policing and the legal system. It would be around this time, about five years after this event, that protests against racial bias in police killings of unarmed Black men and other people of color would just begin to become widely covered in mainstream media in the 21st century.[6] Whether as a result of my own consciousness raising or merely as a result of media saturation, either way, I began to think that racial bias was the most likely explanation for why my friend was assumed perpetrator and me victim. After all, I'm of a mixed, mostly eastern European heritage, while my friend is of mixed heritage with an Irish American mom and a dad from the Yakima nation, one of the largest tribes in Washington state (Office of Financial Management, 2011).

More than a decade later, to prepare for this book, that same friend and I were talking about this memory, and I told him that the only explanation I could think of was racial bias, and how horrible I thought it was that the police treated him that way. My friend, to my total surprise, first offered to "be my Juicy Smalls for this book",[7] and then went on to explain how he felt compelled to tell me he's convinced a more likely explanation is that the car we hit with candy earlier that night either called off a tip in retaliation, or just saw us running away and leaped to a lot of conclusions. He insisted, because the cop told him as he was being searched that they had an exact description of him as the perpetrator, that it seemed unlikely it was a biased and/or a spur of the moment choice on behalf of the officer.

He makes a good point, though that then makes me wonder about whoever called in the tip, and how they saw the event, and again why they assumed he was the one threatening me even though I had (back then as teenagers anyway) 7 inches and 30 pounds on him. My friend says that doesn't matter (he forgets how much stronger I was back then, obviously) and it's because after we ran off after hitting the car he yelled something at me and I ran faster. Definitely could be, can't say I really know, and he makes a good point.

Native American disparities in the criminal legal system

The arguments for racial bias being a cause—that a cop in the Pacific Northwest could have acted with bias toward a kid with visible Native American heritage, especially in areas where Native Americans are one of the largest racial minority groups—is hardly a stunning claim, even if it doesn't apply in my case. Although neglected in conversations around police violence and criminal legal system reform nationally in America, there is no shortage of stories and research that supports this claim (Hansen, 2017). I was once part of a 2015 study in Tacoma, Washington that suggested that depending on the presiding judge, Native Americans were up to 7.5 times more likely to be jailed for misdemeanors than similarly situated [8] White defendants in a small city in Washington state some 30 miles from where my friend and I were stopped by the police (Dunn, Munoz and Taylor, 2018). A 2015 study from South Dakota listing reasons for motor vehicle stops in a county with a large Native American population found that 65% of stops of Native American people were related to driving without a license or insurance with the remainder being related to visible infractions, while in contrast, about 66% of stops for White and Asian people actually referred to visible infractions. The same study, which finds little to no overrepresentation of Native American people relative to White people in traffic stops overall, would find that Native American people were nearly twice as likely to be stopped by police if county level population estimates are relied on as data, though there seems to be ongoing debate among academics about how to measure this.[9]

Maybe more important than anything suggested in the studies above, perhaps the most infamous instance of police violence in the Washington state's history was the murder in 2010 of John T. Williams, a 50-year-old, seventh generation Nitinat woodcarver and citizen of the Nuu-Chah-Nulth First Nations. A Seattle Police Department officer saw Williams cross the street in front of his marked police car carrying an open pocket knife and a piece of cedar. After noticing the knife, the officer left his vehicle, approached Williams from behind, and ordered him three times to drop the knife. Perhaps unbeknownst to the officer, Williams was carrying the tools of his trade and hearing impaired, and presumably not able to hear the officer's orders. Thus, when Williams failed to respond to the officer within 4 seconds, the officer fired his weapon five times from 10 feet away. Williams was struck by four bullets and died at the scene. While the initial police report described Williams as menacing, later eyewitness testimony would contradict this (Capitol Hill Seattle, 2011; Renville, 2011). These events would become the start of a large investigation into racially biased policing and excessive use of force by the Seattle Police Department that would eventually result in the consent decree the department remains under more than a decade later (MacDonald Hoauge & Bayless, 2018).

Zooming out to national statistics, the shooting of John T. Williams can be seen as part of a larger pattern of the higher likelihood of police violence being exerted against Native American people relative to White people or other groups. Although official government sources for police violence are limited, using data aggregated from media reports from the Mapping Police Violence project found Native Americans to be 1.7 times more likely than White people to be killed by police between 2013 and June 2022, and while this is lower than the nearly three times greater risk for Black Americans in the same time period, it remains a large disparity.[10] Furthermore, these national statistics obscure a much more extreme portion of the story. If we look at the ratio of police killing of Native Americans to White people in the states with some of largest Native American populations in the Central Mountain West, Pacific Northwest, and Alaska, we observe much larger disparities. For example, in the same time period, Native American people were up to 11.9 times more likely than White people to be killed by police in North Dakota, and 4.5 times more likely than White people to be killed by police in Washington state (see Fig. 1 for more details).[11] Additionally, 424 out of 10,169 or about 4% of violent police encounters documented by Mapping Police Violence occurred within 10 miles of a reservation, whereas only an estimated 0.5%–1% of the US population lives on or within 10 miles of reservation, suggesting that people who live on or within 10 miles of a reservation are between 4 and 8 times more likely than the rest of the US population to be a victim of police violence.[12]

Different treatment: law enforcement

At the risk of doing too much extrapolating from national statistics, let's briefly return from the macro to the personal, to instances of police bias and violence near my hometown, which may more clearly illustrate instances of differential treatment when entering the criminal legal system through interaction

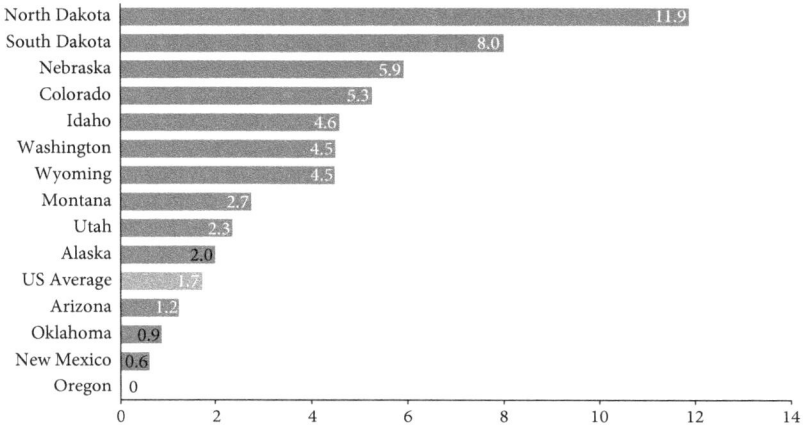

Figure 1 Ratio of Native American to White police deaths per one million people, by US state, 2013–2022.

with the police. Much more recent to the relatively low-key story of me and my friend, in May of 2015, not far from the exact spot my friend and I were stopped, two young Black men ages 21 and 24 were shot in the back after attempting to shoplift beer from a local supermarket. According to local reporting, the two men, Andre Thompson and Bryson Chaplain, entered the supermarket in the early morning and attempted to leave without paying with a case of beer. They were confronted by the clerk working that night, at which point they threw the case at her before fleeing. Immediately after, they fled into the woods surrounding a nearby skate park, where the officer dispatched to respond attempted to engage them. The official police report claims the officer identified himself and ordered the two men to sit down, at which point one of them began to advance toward him with a skateboard overhead. At this juncture, the officer opened fire, striking one of the two men in the arm, at which point they fled again. The report states that the officer then pursued the two deeper into the woods, eventually engaged them again, and fired, striking both of them. Both were in critical condition after the gunshot wounds, and one is now paralyzed from the waist down (Carter, 2015; O'Sullivan, 2015).

In contrast to the police officer's account of the story, in a 2018 interview, one of the men described that the officer began advancing toward them before starting to shoot and before engaging with either one of them. Additional testimony by forensics experts indicates that key physical and photographic evidence does not line up with the officer's version of events. Nevertheless, the trial did not end in Andre and Bryson's favor. Andre was sentenced to 2 months in county jail and Bryson was sentenced to 10 months in county jail with extra time added for throwing the case of beer at the store clerk (Radovsky, 2018).

Of all the reasons to be outraged by this story (and there are many to pick from) not the least of them should be the vast number of young White men (including the author) who have shoplifted the very same type of goods from that very same store, and did not end up with any jail time, let alone being shot at multiple times. Not only have I committed exactly this same crime at exactly this same place, but I could probably give the names of five other White men who have done exactly this same thing at exactly this same store between the ages of 18 and 24 (the prime age and crime curve timing, for you aspiring criminologists out there) and had never been so much as stopped by an employee, let alone shot. Not that stealing beer is ever a defensible activity, but surely living in a society where the punishment for a petty crime can be such a violent altercation is not the world we want to live in.

That Andre and Bryson were stopped for behavior that falls somewhere between similar and identical behavior, for which I and other "similarly situated" White men were not stopped for, fits a broader pattern in policing, and one that some researchers believe has changed during the same period that American policing experienced a large wave of changes. One study from Weaver et al. compared cohorts of Black and White youth with both self-reported criminal and arrest behavior in the late 1970s and 1990s (Weaver, Papachristos and Zanger-Tishler, 2019). Weaver et al. find that after controlling for a range of socioeconomic factors, in 1979, the probability of arrest was virtually identical for Black and White respondents with similar self-reported criminal behavior, whereas for the 1997 cohort, the probability of arrest for both groups increased dramatically for Black respondents relative to White respondents. In other words, their results suggest that White youth would need to commit considerably more self-reported crime than Black youth to face the probability of arrest. The authors argue that the difference between these two cohorts is no coincidence, as they argue this coincides with clear turns of expanded police oversight and punishment.

Compelling as the results of Weaver et al. may seem, it is only one study. In another study by Neil and Sampson, in 2021, the authors critique the analysis in Weaver et al. for not containing any data for those born past 1984, and furthermore, relies only on self-reported data (Neil and Sampson, 2021). Reconciling this critique is a challenging task and outside the scope of this book. Still, limitations aside, the results of Weaver et al. at least suggest some empirical validation that changes in the likelihood of arrest for illegal behavior has not increased proportionally between Black and White youth over the last 50 years.

***

The differential treatment that racial discrimination against Black drivers and pedestrians results in more stops and searches (and thus potentially more arrests) has become one of the more widely covered issues of the last 10 years, at least as far as news coverage of the Black Lives Matter movement has extended that conversation. While many studies have been written on this topic[13], likely the largest in terms of sample size, comes from the Stanford Open Policing Project, which analyzed about 255 million stops carried out by a total of 56 police departments across the US. The authors of the Stanford study find that Black drivers are more likely to be stopped and more likely to be searched than White drivers, and that importantly, this gap declines in situations where the officer is unable to ascertain the driver's race (Pierson et al., 2020). The outcomes of more stops and searches for Black Americans may be unsurprisingly correlated with greater likelihood of experiencing police violence, where for example a 2015 study assessing racial bias in police shootings by Cody T. Ross of the University of California, found that unarmed Black Americans were about 3.5 times more likely than unarmed White Americans to be shot by the police. Ross also critically finds these risk ratios increased in areas with larger Black populations and greater socioeconomic inequality but had no relationship to crime rates after controlling for these covariates (Ross, 2015). This suggests a possibility that to some extent police policy in terms of where to prioritize certain resources, may in part explain some of the gaps we see in Black and White arrest gaps and police violence gaps, even net of controlling for differences in socioeconomic inequality.

While studies like the Stanford Open Policing Project may represent some of the largest studies ever done on potential biased police traffic behavior, implicit discretionary bias is only a part of what potentially drives differences in treatment for similar or same behavior, which ultimately leads to different outcomes in the criminal legal system. Real, stated differences in terms of how to handle different behaviors based on the location they occur, and the perceived risk factors of people observed may have drastically different outcomes in terms of arrest and thus future documented criminal history and risk for people living in different places.

To look at things from another angle, in America's urban counties, racial disparities in prison admissions between Black and White people are tightly correlated with the disparity in the proportion of population living below the federal poverty line (FPL). To illustrate this, we can compare data from the Bureau of Justice Statistics on prison admission population rates by race with the proportion of the population living below the FPL by race as reported by the US census. In 2016, the latest year for which data were available at the time of this writing, prison admission rates for Black people living in urban counties in America ranged from 127 to 1,430 per 100,000 Black people ages 15–64. In contrast, the prison admission rates for White people ranged from 5 to 350 per 100,000 White people ages 15–64. There is not a single urban county in America where proportionally more White people than Black people were admitted to prison, but the extent of this disparity varies enormously, as does the gap in those who are below the FPL. For example, if we compare official reporting from the Bureau of Justice Statistics and US Census data in Jefferson County (Birmingham), Alabama, Black people are about twice as likely to be admitted to prison as White people, and about 2.8 times more likely to have had an income under the federal poverty level (FPL) in the last year. In contrast, in Hennepin County Minnesota (Minneapolis), Black people are about 15 times more likely to be admitted to prison than White people, and about 5 times more likely to have had an income under the FPL in the last year.[14]

There are, of course, many ways to measure inequality in society and the FPL is only one imperfect choice among many. Therefore, a preoccupation with this is to some extent reductive. Nevertheless, the relationship between the gap in the proportion of the population below the FPL and prison admissions rates between Black and White people in urban counties in America is correlated, with a Pearson's correlation of about 0.45 up to 0.55 if one outlier (San Francisco County, California) is omitted. See Fig. 2 for more information.

To be fair, focusing police resources in some areas over others may make perfect sense—crime is after all much higher in some areas. These areas, in America, anyway, are almost universally poorer areas, which particularly in America's cities often means areas with proportionally larger populations of Black and Hispanic people. That research like Ross's found a relationship between socioeconomic inequality and police violence does not exist in a vacuum, and other studies have found a correlation with other forms of interpersonal violence as well. In fact, a series of studies going at least as far back as the 1990s through to the early 2000s

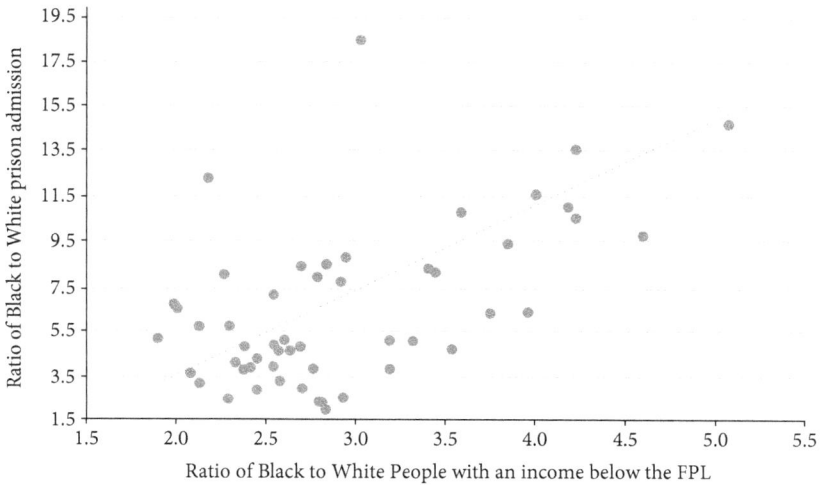

Figure 2 Ratio of Black and White prison admission rates vs. ratio of Black and White people living at or below the FPL, 2016. The ratio of prison admissions among Black and White non-Hispanic people ages 15–64 in 2016 contrasted against the ratio of percent of people living below the federal poverty level (FPL). Demographic data were collected from the US American Community Survey Five-Year Estimates (2012–2016), while prison admission data were collected from the Vera Institute's curated BJS data on incarceration trends (Vera Institute of Justice, 2023). Counties with no prison or census data were omitted, and San Francisco County, California, as outlier with a Black/White prison admission rate ratio of 40.9 and poverty ratio of 3.9, was omitted from the chart for clarity, for a total of 53 out of 63 urban counties in America represented.

have examined differences in Black and White crime rates, and sometimes homicide rates, and frequently identified income inequality, education, and wealth gaps, and other socioeconomic factors as a strong predictor of differences in crime rates, in one case death, by firearm homicide rates or homicide more broadly

(Light and Ulmer, 2016; Siegel et al., 2022; Ulmer, Harris and Steffensmeier, 2012; Velez, Krivo and Peterson, 2003).

This naturally leads to the question of why differences in socioeconomic inequality are associated with differences in crime rates or in some cases violence. A simple explanation of differences in crime rates, or risk of police violence, and its connection to socioeconomic inequality is sometimes depicted as an argument that people with less material resources may be more inclined to turn to crime to meet their needs. While this is a cogent explanation that is undoubtedly true in some instances, more recent scholarship in criminology elaborates on gaps in the theory. For example, Richard Wilkson, an epidemiologist at the University of Nottingham in the UK, elaborates on the extent to which inequality, not real material deprivation, is associated with violence (Wilkson, 2010). As Wilkson puts it, "inequality within a society—rather than the absolute level of income itself—has such a profound impact on violence and the quality of social relations". Drawing on the social determinants of health literature, Wilkson argues that a more unequal society creates more relative deprivation and competition for those resources, fracturing social bonds and increasing exposure to chronic stress, which in turn increases the likelihood of violence.

To illustrate more succinctly the depth of the correlation between criminal legal system exposure and socioeconomic status, we can review a study looking at a cohort of boys born between 1980 and 1986, which found that boys born in the bottom 10% spectrum of household incomes were 20 times more likely to end up in prison then those born in the top 10% (Looney and Turner, 2018). This is even more severe nearer the far ends of the income spectrum. Boys born in the bottom 1% spectrum of household incomes were nearly 40 times more likely to end up in prison than those born in the top 1% (Looney and Turner, 2018).

These findings, while specific to prison admissions, seem consistent with other research from Europe and the UK that finds experiences of childhood poverty and low family income to be very large predictors of future violent behavior or self-harm, or other risk factors for crime (Mok et al., 2018; Ramanathan, Balasubramanian and Faraone, 2017; Wickham et al., 2017). Taking an even broader perspective, in 2003 researchers from the World Bank assessed that a causal link between income inequality and crime rates are positively correlated, even when considering other causes of crime (Fajnzylber, Lederman and Loayza, 2002), though more contemporary research has suggested a nation's welfare state may ameliorate this link (Deshpande and Mueller-Smith, 2022; Savolainen, 2006).

These studies in aggregate suggest that people from the poorest parts of society are more likely to end up arrested or imprisoned. The mechanisms behind this are complicated, reflecting perhaps real differences in economic motivation to commit crime, differences in priorities for police resources that may influence how crimes are handled in a given area, and theorized by some at least, different strains on social relations that exacerbate violence. Complicated as reconciling all of this may be for academics, the takeaway should be clear: if you are someone or somewhere on the losing end of inequality, there's a good chance you're both at greater risk of being a victim of violence as well as being targeted by the criminal legal system (Alliance for Safety and Justice, 2016).

More police where there is more crime

So if greater inequality potentially increases violence and crime, and incarceration potentially ruptures social bonds for individuals further increasing their likelihood of future crime (Agan, Doleac and Harvey, 2022; Leslie and Pope, 2017), why would any government aggressively enforce laws in or against people living in areas at the bottom end of the income distribution? Particularly if incarceration is associated with a further increase in lost wages and wealth that may continue to exacerbate existing inequality (Brown, 2019; Sykes and Maroto, 2016)? A cynical answer may be political control or conspiratorial actions by the police. No doubt there are horrible incidents along these lines that have occurred, and indeed, this was the law of the land for hundreds of years in this country. Certainly, smarter people than me have made a case for this, but I will tell you the answer I have received from law enforcement, and that is echoed among progressive prosecutors and reformers, is that law enforcement resources are targeted to where calls for emergency service to 911 come from and by extension where more crimes are reported (Dawson, 2022; Thacher, 2004). Testing the validity of this statement with calls for service data everywhere is outside the scope of this book, but as indicated in the previous section, crime victimization surveys do seem to underscore that people living areas with lower incomes are more likely to be victims of crime.

Specifically, the 2021 National Crime Victimization Survey (NCVS), a nationally representative victimization survey conducted by Bureau of Justice Statistics found that people 12 years and older, with a household income of less than $25,000, were about 4 times more likely to be a victim of non-simple assault[15] violent crime than people with household incomes of $200,000 or more (Thompson and Tapp, 2022). This is further elaborated in the 2016 Alliance for Safety and Justice Survey of Victims' Views, the only nationally representative survey of crime victims' views on safety and justice. This survey finds that victims are far more likely to be low-income, young, and people of color. Additionally, they find that for many people these are not isolated incidents, where especially violent crime victims are four times as likely to be repeat crime victims of four or more crimes (Alliance for Safety and Justice, 2016). Feelings of safety in a responder's given community also varied significantly by income, race, and gender. Only 38% of low-income people reported feeling "very safe" in their community, relative to 71% of high-income people, and about 35% of Black or Latina women reported feeling "very safe" in their community, relative to 54% of White men (Alliance for Safety and Justice, 2016).

For me, as a White man who feels, and probably is, very safe, and perhaps for those of us who didn't grow up in areas where crime is high, and who have, at most, been the victim of a very minor crime, if ever at all, what it means to feel unsafe in the community we live can be a hard point to truly understand. I have had in my life, through working as a criminal legal system researcher, the chance to meet people who have devoted their entire lives to attempting to promote safety and justice in their own communities. Often many of the folks I have met have come from some of the most deprived areas of America, and a huge part of their drive to devote their lives to this work is to promote safety and justice in their own communities.

Reconciling this tension, where people with the least amount of socioeconomic advantage are both at the greatest risk of being a victim of crime, and of, in turn, being brought into the criminal legal system is far outside the scope of this book. However, one potential theoretical framework that may help reconcile this is called situational action theory or SAT. As a theory of crime, SAT argues that criminal behavior is a function of individual moral perceptions about what is right and wrong, the sense of whether there is an alternative choice available to them, and critically, the extent of how often a person is exposed to the sorts of situations where criminal behavior is a possibility (Centre for Analytic Criminology, 2023). For example, a young person living in a neighborhood in which as a student they face a risk of being mugged on their way home from school clearly faces a higher risk of victimization. If they find themselves in that situation, self-defense may easily lead to a violent altercation that leads to subsequent criminal legal involvement and all the repercussions that entails. Regardless of whether they ever are called up to defend themselves like this, the young person might alter their behavior to be more outwardly aggressive to try to avoid being targeted in the first place, which may in turn increase the risk of future violent altercations with others, increasing their risk in direct response to their conditions. A young person who faces no perception of this kind of risk clearly has a much lower risk of victimization or a sort of preemptive response that could get them arrested.

Seen through SAT, we might consider historical and socioeconomic inequalities to be a sort of "causes of causes" of crime (Centre for Analytic Criminology, 2023). In other words, while it is true that a large number of people exposed to the same socioeconomic, historical, or racially biased disadvantage do not go on to commit the same criminal acts, it also true that the inequalities these conditions create in society present an extremely unequal situation, where the random lottery of birth determines how much exposure a given person may have to potential criminal behavior. Combine this with the fact that resources related to enforcement, and tolerance for some illegal behaviors, are not evenly distributed, and SAT as a theory allows for a cogent explanation of inequality seen in both victimization and criminal legal involvement.

***

The choice to prioritize police resources in areas with higher calls for service may not be purely driven by statistics. Some of this likely reflects some of the real preferences of people who live in these areas. If we take New York City as an example, Eric Adams won the 2021 Democratic primary for mayor (New York City has not as of the time of this writing had a republican mayor since 2001, and it was generally assumed whoever won the primary would win the office) on a classic tough on crime message; a message of getting more police on the streets—specifically in the least affluent neighborhoods in New York City with the highest proportions of Black and Brown residents. Not only did Adams win on this message, he won on this message specifically by carrying electoral districts in those neighborhoods, where he won in large margins, while he lost to more progressive candidates avoiding tough on crime messages and vowing to be more critical of police (and especially of their budget) in left leaning, affluent, and Whiter parts of New York City (Smart, Fischer and Krolik, 2021). Similar results were seen in Minneapolis's vote against defunding the police and collapsing the department into a broader public safety department during the protests surrounding the murder of George Floyd (Kanu, 2021).

Although perhaps partially motivated by calls for service, the choice to devote more police resources to a given location often doesn't stop at responding to more calls. In practice, this may mean adopting law enforcement strategies like focused deterrence or the infamous "broken windows policing" to greatly increase the influence of police in the area. In contrast, areas with lower crime rates may see less police presence and thus, lower exposure to arrest or enforcement, particularly of more minor crimes.

To unpack just one example of what this may in practice, "focused deterrence" refers to a collection of interventions and policy choices by police to specifically focus greater police resources (and at times involved referrals to social service programs or community-based organizations) on a relatively small number of people and affiliated networks thought to be responsible for a disproportionate share of crime, often in gangs. In practice, this often means facilitated conversations or messaging to members or group leadership that police will rigorously survey and enforce even the most minor infractions by members and people in their immediate community in an effort to prevent future violent behavior. While early research into the topic showed large reductions in crime, more recent scholarship has shown much more modest gains when higher quality study designs are used. Despite this, the evidence does seem that focused deterrence, particularly for individuals in gangs, is associated with reductions in crime, and remains an option with a strong evidence base that policy makers and police chiefs turn in their attempts of reducing violence (Braga, Weisburd and Turchan, 2019).

Regardless of the effects on crime, often absent from the conversation is the potential collateral consequences of focused deterrence. The recent scholarship of Rachel Swaner and her team at the Center for Court Innovation in New York City found through 287 in-depth interviews with young New York City gang members that a vicious cycle existed in which gang membership was often a solution to the sort of grinding poverty members experienced as a result of their exclusion from mainstream society, and in turn then led to even greater exclusion from society (Swaner, 2022). Considering the potential that even just pretrial detention has on future recidivism (Agan, Doleac and Harvey, 2022; Leslie and Pope, 2017), when applied against only a small and highly vulnerable segment of the population, not to mention the obvious corrosion of trust this facilitates between law enforcement and members of the community, it certainly seems possible that Swaner's conclusions that focused deterrence will not make communities safer in the long run may be legitimate one.

Maximum tolerance: drugs and universities

If focused deterrence is an example of a strategy that employs zero tolerance for any illegal behavior toward a select group of people, then we ought to consider what it looks like when the exact opposite is employed; that is, when a select group of people are deliberately provided the most lenient and forgiving approach. Simon Singer in his 2014 book *America's Safest City* reviewed this difference in terms of "maximum tolerance" for petty criminal behavior in predominantly White New York City suburbs, relative to zero tolerance in poor neighborhoods. If we think back to the findings of Weaver et al., who estimated that young White people needed to typically engage in much higher rates of criminal behavior to result in arrest than young Black people (Weaver, Papachristos and Zanger-Tishler, 2019), we can see these findings, to some extent, as a real world reflection of the difference between living in a maximum and a zero tolerance area.

Perhaps nowhere is the difference between maximum tolerance and zero tolerance clearer than if we review the difference in how college campus security and police handle drug and weapons offenses relative to what we know are the experiences of people targeted by focused deterrence. If America's prisons show stark overrepresentation of people born in the poorest parts of society, America's universities, and in particular elite private universities, show almost the exact opposite representation. According to the Harvard-based Opportunity Insights, in a 2017 *New York Times* article, prospective high school students from the top one-tenth of 1% of household incomes were nearly 50 times more likely than students from the bottom 25% of household incomes to attend an elite school (Aisch et al., 2017).

College campuses, of course, are filled primarily with people between the ages of 18–24, prime crime committing years if the age crime curve and conventional criminology wisdom is correct (National Institute of Justice, 2014). Additionally, despite large shifts over the last several decades, college campuses, in general, continue to have an overrepresentation of White, middle or upper class people (Jez, 2008; Monarrez and Washington, 2020; Pfeffer, 2018). This suggests a strong potential that many young people in their prime crime committing years may be sorted in the case of college institutions, in part, by their socioeconomic status into places that are much more lenient than the rest of society and certainly relative to policing in high crime neighborhoods.

This certainly resonates for me as a White person, who from the ages of 15 to 22, spent most of his time in a "safe" middle-class community or on college campuses. Almost all the illegal behavior I've committed in my life, including possessing and being complicit in the sale of felony narcotics, occurred during these years of my life. In fact, as described in the introduction, my first arrest for this was on a college campus, and resulted in my immediate referral to treatment, with no booking into jail, despite being found to be in possession of multiple felony counts of narcotics and drug paraphernalia.

Referral to treatment without jail seems to be a relatively common outcome for someone like me who was arrested on a college campus. To provide some empirical illustration of this, we can review data from the US Department of Education's Campus Safety and Security statistics database, which provides data on arrests and disciplinary actions across America (US Department of Education, 2017). According to this data, from 2007 to 2015, an already present gap between the number of drug offense-related disciplinary actions and arrests grew sharply. Specifically, for all institutions, there were approximately 27% to 56% more drug-related disciplinary actions than drug-related arrests from 2007 to 2015, suggesting that a very large proportion of drug

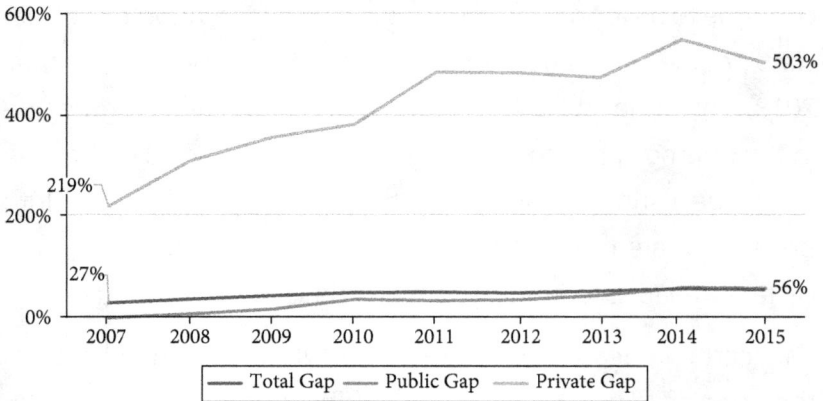

Figure 3 Percent difference between drug offense disciplinary actions and arrests at US higher education institutions, 2007–2015.

"incidents" on college campuses did not result in an arrest. Gaps for public four-year institutions track all institutions nearly identically, while gaps for private nonprofit four-year institutions are much larger, with 219% to 503% more drug-related disciplinary events than arrests from 2007 to 2015. For private nonprofit universities, these differences are similarly present for illegal weapons possession. For example, in 2015, in contrast to public universities where there were 44% fewer illegal weapons possession disciplinary actions than arrests, in the same year in private nonprofit universities there were 59% more disciplinary actions than arrests for illegal weapons possession. See Figs. 3 and 4 below for more information.

To some extent, these campus trends reflect a larger pattern of declining drug arrests across the United States from 2009 to 2019. Analysis by the Pew Charitable Trusts show that even as drug arrests, almost all of which are for drug possession, have remained relatively constant over the last decade, drug-related

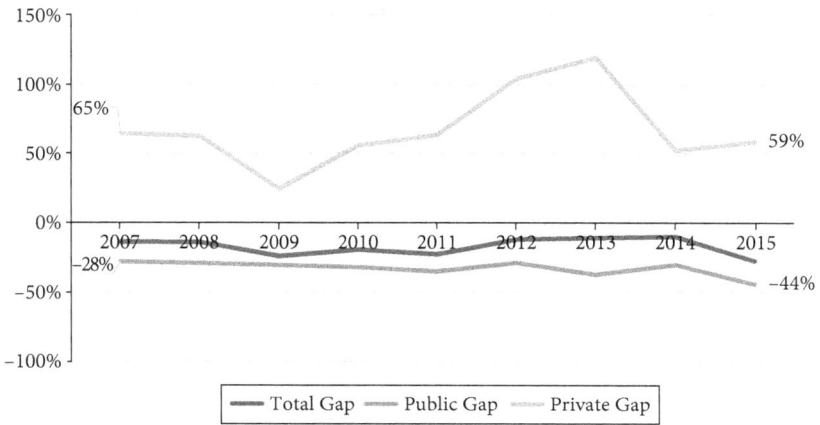

Figure 4 Percent difference between illegal weapon possession disciplinary actions and arrests at US higher education institutions, 2007–2015.

prison admissions have declined 33% on average, with very large regional variation by state, particularly in more progressive states with more alternatives to incarceration for these crimes (Pew Charitable Trusts, 2022). This may mean, the gaps we see in university disciplinary actions and arrests reflect universities acting as more progressive institutions, in other words handling drug offenses or weapons possession in a way that many on the political left wish would be extended to everyone. To illustrate the attitude of university officials clearly, one official, following a high-profile arrest of students at Wesleyan University, defended their approach of notably lower arrests than disciplinary actions by saying:

> We are committed to responding to violations with education, treatment and sanctions, as appropriate. These federal statistics reflect our vigorous efforts

> to enforce our policies. At Wesleyan, we don't sweep these problems under the rug.
>
> (New, 2015)

Whether or not progressive reform is the intention of university officials, this gap between students and all other young people, and especially young people who live in areas with focused deterrence, nevertheless suggests the existence of a different tier of punishment for these types of offenses, depending on if the young person is a student, and particularly an elite student, or not. In other words, depending on where they are in their lives, young people will face drastically different experiences for very similar behavior.

Imagine for a second if college neighborhoods, share houses, Greek houses, dormitories, quads, or whatever term you like for places full of young college adults, were policed the same way as poor neighborhoods. Imagine, if like in neighborhoods targeted by police enforcement, residents of colleges were randomly stopped and searched and "known associates" of "known offenders" were regularly harassed on every minor infraction possible as a pretense for a stop and search. Do you think we might see an uptick in felony drug possession and sexual assault statistics in college campuses and neighborhoods then? What about minor crimes, such as driving with a suspended license, driving without insurance, or shoplifting?

Maximum tolerance: retail theft and wage theft

That law enforcement resources are concentrated in areas where there are higher levels of interpersonal crime, that is crime committed by one person to another whether that's theft or more serious violence, seems undeniable to me. Many people believe that there should be low tolerance for and swift responses to crimes of interpersonal violence, and it's not hard to understand why that is. However, thinking of crime only as something that occurs between individual people can ignore a large amount of behavior that ultimately has many victims, and for this type of behavior, there seems to be more tolerance. For example, there is no jurisdiction I know of where crimes such as wage theft by employers, or housing discrimination by landlords, is counted as any part of conventional crime statistics.

To elaborate with a quick example, we can contrast differences in how retail theft and wage theft are addressed within the framework of maximum or minimum tolerance. Both retail theft and wage theft crimes may be rarely enforced, but the former still warrants a call to the police in many people's opinions, the results of which can be quite severe if we reflect on Andre and Bryson's experience. Of course, in people's eyes the reason for enforcing petty theft charges is that it is still a theft in which someone is taking something of value causing a loss to a business or another person. Because there is no comprehensive reporting mechanism or data available for retail losses from theft, and because these statistics are often passionately invoked in political arguments about how to respond to crime, estimating total losses from retail theft across the country for any given year is a politically fraught and challenging task. One estimate by the National Retail Federation, the world's largest retail trade association, estimated $17.08 billion dollars in retail theft losses to shoplifting, with $2.1 billion in organized retail theft, in the United States in 2020 (National Retail Federation, 2021). In contrast, the Retail Industry Leaders Association estimated there was $68 billion in retail theft losses in US in the same year, though reporting from the Los Angeles Times indicates some industry experts consider the Retail Industry Leaders Association estimates unreliable (Dean, 2021).[16] Staggeringly high as these amounts may sound, it's worth considering that these estimates suggest that retail theft represents between 0.07% and 2% of profits from sales in the same year, according to analysis from the Los Angeles Times. Considering the relatively low proportion of losses these account for, it is unsurprising, as reporting from the Los Angeles Times indicates, that many stores choose to maintain security with a non-pursuit policy and generally assess that the cost of enforcement to be greater than the losses recovered (Dean, 2021). Despite this, organized retail theft continues to receive extensive media exposure with some interest groups lobbying for harsher penalties.

In contrast, reporting on wage theft in America is comparatively uncommon and rarely captures the public eye. One 2017 report from the Economic Policy Institute (EPI) making use of the US Census Current Population Survey estimated that in America's ten most populous states alone, only one type of wage theft, minimum wage violations, accounted for more than $8 billion in losses to workers annually, or about $3,300 per worker per year (Cooper and Kroeger, 2017). Not only is that approximately

6 times higher than National Retail Federation's estimate of $2.1 billion in losses due to organized retail theft, in effect that works out to nearly 25% of the annual earnings that federal minimum wage workers would have been entitled to. Furthermore, this is almost certainly a conservative estimate of wage theft. For one, it includes only minimum wage violations, and does not include other common forms of wage theft such as misclassification of workers as independent contractors or failing to pay overtime. Additionally, one study estimates that as many as 98% of low wage, private sector, nonunion employees subject to forced arbitration, do not report wage theft out of fear of employer retaliation (Baran and Campbell, 2021). While challenging to enumerate, this surely suggests that reported wage thefts are at best undercounted.

***

Before concluding this section on maximum and zero tolerance, I'll give one more anecdote from my own life. Recall from the introduction that, I ran into several people I knew from growing up while in jail after I was arrested. Though all of us had in common varying degrees of substance-abuse problems, our backgrounds otherwise ran a wide range. As I mentioned, one person I knew who had grown up in foster care later suffered a fatal overdose almost immediately after joining the same diversion program as me. In contrast, I also ran into a friend who was a relatively privileged White person, a son of a doctor and former college student, who was now an opioid addict heroin dealer and gang member (complete with affiliation tattoo and a history of violence). This same friend ended up enrolled in the same diversion program as me but was only able to enroll in the program after prosecutors dropped an illegal firearm charge filed against him that would have otherwise disqualified him from diversion and sent him to prison. Mind you, the firearm was his, and the choice to drop the charge, at least from his account, seemed to be much more about allowing him to participate in the program after his private defense spoke with the prosecution. A truly eerie resemblance to a story that Michelle Alexander describes in her book *The New Jim Crow*, where a colleague asks her to drop a gun charge against a young White man who was stopped by police and found to be in possession of drugs and a hunting rifle. In her book, Alexander states that her colleague argued "it's not like he's a gun-toting drug dealer", even if that is quite literally what he was (Alexander, 2010).

Conclusion

What then does all of this mean for differences in treatment for entering the criminal legal system? At the most extreme ends for young people, a two-tiered system is in play, where the most affluent (or even just the more affluent) of society, who are much more likely to be White, have more off-ramps from punishment in the criminal legal system and all its subsequent collateral consequences. If, in fact, they are even punished at all, which may not be in the case for many minor crimes (Bhutta et al., 2020). When young people are given more lenient treatment, this is seemingly in part due to the combination of living in low crime areas or attending an institution with a forgiving attitude toward punishment. And White young people may be even less likely to be targeted on the basis of their skin tone. In contrast, people at the bottom tier of incomes in some of the most deprived parts of the country are punished more frequently and deliberately because of where they live. As a result, they are subject to all the collateral consequences of traditional punishment, in an effort to reduce the very real greater risk of violence they already face in their community, facilitated in part by socioeconomic inequality, which may be only furthered following exposure to arrest and incarceration (Agan, Doleac and Harvey, 2022; Brown, 2019; Gordon et al., 2021; Leslie and Pope, 2017).

Of course, this is not a simple story. The justification for this difference in treatment is often genuinely rooted in what I believe is a real desire among not just conventional actors but progressive actors and community members to make communities safer. In fact, it is seemingly a paradox that almost everywhere in the US, the same communities that experience the disproportionate brunt of incarceration and criminal legal system involvement are those that experience the greatest amount of street-level interpersonal violence and criminal victimization. There is no easy solution to this that I can see. I can't imagine it will ever be a successful message to say to people who themselves or whose family members have been victims of violence that there will be less police presence or response, not more, and what we need is a multigenerational solution, for which there is no political will, and even if there was political will, it may take 10 years to make a difference, and we're sorry you're hurting now. There can be no ignoring that being a victim of crime has both immediate and long-lasting repercussions, and it's no wonder then that people want to feel safer now and will support investment in greater law enforcement resources.

However, to whatever extent the views of victims in the Alliance for Safety and Justice's 2016 survey are representative of all crime victims, it is the case that many of these people, while fearing for their safety, prefer to see investments made outside the criminal legal system. The same survey reports that victims of crime are 15 times more likely to prefer investments in schools and education over jails and prison, and 4 times more likely to prefer investments in drug treatment over prisons and jails. According to a report summarizing the survey, these views are consistent across demographics related to age, gender, race, and political party affiliation (Alliance for Safety and Justice, 2016).

Yet, despite investment outside of the criminal legal system being the preference of many of the very people who justify harsher responses to crime, it seems that if current practices continue, we will also continue to see a pattern where when interacting with police, the majority of people's first entrance into the criminal legal system, the most privileged are much more likely to receive lenient treatment. Whether this is because they're in a place or institution that while "not sweeping things under the rug" certainly doesn't punish as usual or because they're on the winning side of racial bias. On the other side, the least well off in society will receive harsher treatment, either because they live somewhere where police are literally instructed to be stricter, or because they are on the losing side of racial bias, or very likely both. The repercussions of this difference in treatment can span an individual's entire life in addition to the immediate effects on them in the short term. Furthermore, as we will examine in the next chapter, once arrested and given some kind of disposition, be it incarceration, diversion, probation or otherwise, preexisting differences in socioeconomic resources will continue to influence the experiences of people under criminal legal supervision.

2
During

Learning objectives

- To gain introductory knowledge of "risk, responsivity, and need" as a means of evaluating people's propensity for future offending and how that influences alternative program design, with an eye toward how prior inequality may particularly influence the "need" part.
- To gain introductory knowledge of the concept of "spaces of lawlessness" as a postcolonial legal framework that helps to stitch together an otherwise disparate collection of ways people impacted by the criminal legal system can be mistreated.
- To gain knowledge about ways in which criminal records and prior inequality can influence hiring after arrest and release, and understand the current US national conversation around "banning the box".

Eric was a stout, maybe 5 ft 8 in Black man in his thirties, who was so obese, to borrow an expression from a friend in south Brooklyn, you might say he was easier to go over than around. The first time I met Eric he tried to explain to me why I shouldn't be so hard on prison Nazis:

> Because, look, most of these guys, they have no education, rough lives, they end up in the system very young and stay there for years. Life sometimes. They're just trying to find themselves, man.

For reasons I barely understand, this wasn't the first time somebody felt compelled to tell me this about prison nazis. Small-town Pacific Northwest is not a place known for its demographic diversity in any sense of that phrase, and so frequently I found myself to be the sole Jewish person in cliques in sketchy, predominately White places. In these scenes, if for some reason my ethnicity came up, many people felt compelled to give me a questionable defense of prison nazis for reasons I have to think are usually a little more personal than they wanted to admit to me.

Eric's defense of prison nazis was a new one for me though. For context: we were talking about "these guys" shortly after a mandated session of group "moral reconation therapy", where Eric had brought up how he had recently reconnected with his Catholic roots, prompting a Native American longshoreman in the group to talk about his own new found connection with the spirituality he was raised with, and me to share my cynicism about going to synagogue as a kid. This, for whatever reason, elicited a lot of curiosity on Eric's behalf, and is why we got to talking over cigarettes and vape pens while waiting for the bus after the session.

Eric told me at this time about how, in addition to returning to Catholicism, he had recently reconnected with his school age child, was a few months clean off heroin for the first time in a long time (though definitely not the first time), and was crediting quite a bit of this to his belief in a higher power he'd found through his new (but also old) religion. Eric had a job, was making progress in the diversion program, and seemingly had all the markers of a success story, though those who know better would hesitate to label his progress a success having seen near success stories for junkies in a position like his devolve quickly and unexpectedly before.

Sometime later, maybe a month after our conversation, Eric missed a random urine analysis (UA) required by the program. In this particular program, a missed or late UA was considered the same as a having a positive test, for which the punishment was a short mandatory stay in jail, for somewhere between one and seven days, depending on how many times a participant missed or tested positive on a UA, and how many "clean days" had passed since their last missed or positive test. I don't know if Eric skipped the UA because he relapsed, if he genuinely missed it for a good reason, or if he was simply late that day. All three of those scenarios were common among participants in the program, the author not excluded. Regardless of whatever the reason for missing his UA was, the outcome was going to be the same: Eric was going to jail on a short sanction. Annoying, frightening, enough time to be physically or sexually assaulted, but by anybody's estimate, a hell of lot better than prison or any more time in jail. He would then restart the program from where he left off, though the clock counting his "clean days" from drugs would start over at zero, which would delay his progress through the program and extend his time under court supervision. Overall, this type of punishment, while arguably harsh, would be short enough a period to barely register when measuring jail population rates, and delivered in a quick and consistent manner, which, as we will see in later sections, is considered a best practice for reducing recidivism.

As a very obese man, Eric suffered from sleep apnea and was supposed to sleep with a continuous positive airway pressure (CPAP) machine, the sort of thing that helps you breathe if you stop breathing when you're asleep. I don't know if he simply didn't have one, didn't attempt to take the machine with him for such a short stay in jail, or did attempt to take it but was unable to get the machine approved by jail medical staff in time, but the point is he didn't have the machine with him when he was booked into jail. As an aside: choosing not to take the machine for a short stay, or trying, but being unable to get it approved, is not at all an unlikely outcome in places where for nonurgent matters it can take well over 24 hours for an inmate to see a nurse to confirm the use of the medication or medical devices inmates are entitled to. Regardless, Eric went to spend a short stay in jail for missing a UA, an outcome considered lenient by the powers that be and frankly also by many participants in the diversion program and the local 12-step community, who had done much more serious time than 24 hours in jail.

That night Eric died of complications related to a lack of oxygen caused by his sleep apnea. What is perhaps most remarkable is just how little this seemed to register to anyone running the program or who was a participant in the program. In fact, to seemingly everyone involved, at the time myself included, this didn't seem to elicit anything other than a taciturn and resigned sadness about the situation. I remember, talking to my then narcotics anonymous sponsor about it, and he simply said:

> The most natural thing for an addict to do is die, that's
> why we're here.
>
> (Anonymous, 2012)

Horrified as I was by his statement, my sponsor seemed to have tapped into something about the general attitude, as after all there was no media outcry, no investigation as far as I know, and no seemingly significant attention paid to this. The prevailing attitude was to acknowledge this was sad, but to treat this as some inevitable consequence to be lived with, as one of the many sad things that makes life hard sometimes.

Risk, responsivity, and need

Deaths in custody are rarely seen as preventable by default and only the more unusual cases ever seem to make the news. In 2011, around the time Eric died, approximately 960 people died in jails according to the Bureau of Justice Statistics (Carson, 2021a). In 2019, at least over half of these deaths were attributable to illness, as Eric's may have been. To some it may seem inevitable, after all jails are not responsible for the health behaviors of the people they incarcerated prior to them ever being booked into jail, and chronic health conditions certainly seem to be more common among people who get arrested than those who don't (Nowotny, Rogers and Boardman, 2017). However, we should note that just under 40% of all deaths that occurred in jails in 2019 occurred during the first 7 days of a person's incarceration (Carson, 2021a). This suggests that there may be quite a few other people like Eric, who died of illness, exacerbated by their very literal condition of being incarcerated, whose death was hardly inevitable.

Varied though the reasons any death in custody might be, it is, at the very least, seemingly likely that Eric's incarceration on a short jail sanction increased his risk of death. One might ask why on earth he was sent to jail at all then, if this was a potential risk and the behavior in question was relatively mild. The answers to this likely come from the framework of reasoning that would justify the use of a zero-tolerance jail sanction for something like missing a UA. Sometimes called "swift and certain", sometimes called "saliency", this is often grounded in the idea that assurance of being caught is a more effective deterrent of behavior than is the severity of the punishment. In other words, guaranteeing that if you're late to a UA that it's counted as positive, resulting in a 1–7-day jail sentence, may be a more effective deterrent than only the potential of jail under some circumstances. Zooming out, briefly it'll be beneficial for us to look at the academic literature that accompanies this framework, sometimes called the literature on "what works" (Latessa, Johnson and Koetzle, 2013).

In their 2013 book, Latessa and colleagues provide an excellent summary of the research and history of studying different approaches to reducing recidivism in America. It's a heroic effort, and worth noting as they describe in the early chapters, that for many years the conventional wisdom was treated as "nothing works", and it's a credit in some ways to diligent research and continued pushes for policy change that this outlook has changed. Many things that are credited for "what works" are swift and certain responses to violating program rules. That is, a violation will have a quick punishment, and that punishment is guaranteed and not subject to occasional enforcement.

A core set concept from Latessa's in "what works" for reducing recidivism is that any program attempting to reduce recidivism should consider the "risk", "need", and "responsivity" of its participants with respect to the program. The first or "risk" principle refers to how great of an actual risk is a given person for recidivism. People with more prosocial behaviors, such as "having more friends who don't get into trouble", have a history of secure employment, and have finished at least high school are documented as being lower risk. The second or "need" principle refers to what people need to be able to be in compliance with the program. Transportation, housing, and programming in their own language, are all straightforward examples. The third or "responsivity" principle reflects a person's ability to get something from the program, or respond to it. Clear examples might include people with substance dependency responding to a substance-abuse related program as opposed to other programming, while more abstract examples might include culturally tailored options.

Each of these categories can create different experiences of a reform program for people of different social positions. Perhaps most literally, in their 2013 book Latessa et al. cite a large-scale study describing static risk factors for recidivism, which include literally "lower class origin", personal distress, and family origins among some of the larger risk factors. These are then correlated with dynamic risk factors, some of which can be realistically targeted through programming and some of which are very much outside the scope of any program to address in an equitable way (Latessa, Johnson and Koetzle, 2013).

For example, "bad stress management" or "poor problem solving or coping skills" is associated with greater recidivism, and realistically, behavioral intervention can help a person to develop these (Latessa, Johnson and Koetzle, 2013). Unfortunately, other dynamic risk factors including having a job and "being happy with a job", might be more challenging for a program to address. Surely a good program can help individuals to find a job in places with a strong economy, but changing the type of jobs available to program participants, such that a middle-aged man with little to no work history, who a third-party background check shows as having pending identity theft charges, could realistically get a fulfilling and well-paying job, is quite the challenge.

Similar factors are the case with the "need" principle. In jurisdictions without public transportation, where the bus comes every 30 minutes to every 3 hours, depending on the day, clearly participants with a vehicle will be better positioned for success than those without, and that will almost certainly be to the benefit of participants with more resources. Participants with dependents and many other financial needs will certainly be more challenged to comply with the program as well. The list could continue ad infinitum, and to whatever extent it is not addressed by a program, it will almost certainly show a parallel inequity in who is successful in the program.

Spaces of lawlessness

Subjecting people to rules they cannot realistically comply with due to an unmet need, or else neglecting the safety of people while incarcerated, is not only clearly a violation of "responsivity" principles, but it also exemplifies what Val Napoleon describes as spaces of "lawlessness" within colonial law (Napoleon, 2022). That is, to use Napoleon's definition, any space "where there is unchecked power over the lives of vulnerable people", which seems to inevitably lead to a disregard for their rights to not be harmed or otherwise treated unfairly. This proves to be a useful framework for uniting similar mistreatments of people in the criminal legal system, which vary from everything from a disregard for their time in delays in case processing, to wrongful conviction.

Deaths in custody, such as that which ended Eric's life, are particularly extreme examples of this. Perhaps equally stark and clear are what are sometimes called "miscarriages of justice" or wrongful conviction, or put simply, when people are wrongfully accused and convicted of crimes they did not commit. After all, there is perhaps no more literal failure of any legal system than one that punishes people for crimes others committed.

Ironically, for people not facing prison sentences and instead shorter stints in jail, who end up detained pretrial for weeks or months before hearings or a trial, are effectively treated as though they're guilty prior to a disposition resulting in a release for time served. For people looking at prison sentences, of course, the situation is much more dire. Based on analysis from the national registry of exonerations (UCI Newkirk Center for Science & Society, 2023), people exonerated in 2021 for crimes they did not commit spent an approximate median time of 15 years in prison prior to release.

The implications of wrongful conviction are startlingly disparate between Black and White people. The most recent report from the National Registry of Exoneration, from the University of Michigan, indicates that at least based on the use of existing exoneration data, Black people are seven times more likely than

White people to be innocent of a serious crime of which they've been convicted (Gross et al., 2022). The disparities are much larger for drug crimes. Black people were 19 times more likely to be convicted of drug crime they did not commit, and nearly 9 out of 10 drug crime exonerations stemming from planted drugs from police officers were for Black people (Gross et al., 2022).

While wrongful convictions and subsequent prison and death penalty sentences may be the most extreme examples of unchecked power of and disregard for people in the criminal legal system, much more common is the disregard for the time of individuals in the system—victim or defendant—that occurs as a result of case delay and poor courtroom management. According to a review by the National Center for State Courts released in 2019, 57% of state courts in the participating sample of more than 25 states, failed to resolve felony cases within the national benchmark of 180 days or fewer (Ostrom, Hamblin and Schauffler, 2020). Next to deaths in custody or wrongful conviction, this may seem like a comparatively trivial thing to be concerned with, but when even a single extra day in pretrial detention can raise the risk of an individual being assaulted, losing their employment, losing custody of their kids, and/or any number of other harmful outcomes, prolonged stay due to case delay becomes a much more serious risk. This is particularly egregious when case delay occurs only as a result of arbitrary settings of court hearing dates and bad management.

For perhaps one of the clearest examples of how the enforcement of arbitrary rules can lead to prolonged case processing times; for many years if defendants at Rikers Island in New York City were not taken from their custody at Rikers to the courtroom by 9:30 a.m., they were bumped to the bottom queue of arraignments for the day. The result of this means the defendant may not be seen at all that day, leading to them spending all day shackled in custody in the courtroom just to have their next hearing arbitrarily scheduled for a month out. This despite the fact that nearly all of their capacity to have arrived on time for their arraignment was purely in control of the correctional officers doing the transportation.

This sort of disregard for people's time, if seen as part of a perspective that describes this as a space of "lawlessness", that is, a space where there is unchecked power over vulnerable people, is clearly compatible with one that would book an individual into custody without regard for the medical assistance they may need, such as in the events that led to Eric's death. Missing a UA was considered the same thing as a positive UA, and being a minute late for a UA was considered missing it. Never mind the obvious hypocrisy that court sessions are regularly delayed. This sort of swift, certain, and very strict programming requirement was applied to every aspect of the diversion program, and is indeed to some extent in line with what experts recommend in the "what works" to reduce recidivism academic literature (Latessa, Johnson and Koetzle, 2013). Though certainly it arguably falls short on the "need" side, especially if any concern at all is given to equity.

There are good and intuitive reasons for having a swift and certain approach. Enforcing certain boundaries, as anyone who's ever raised a child, or tried to cultivate a new habit in themselves, or supported a friend trying to change their behavior can tell you, is essential for affecting behavioral change. And changing behavior, of course, is ostensibly why all of us in the diversion program were there after all. However, a completely blind approach to this without consideration for the very real differences individuals have in their capacity to meet these requirements is bound to inevitably advantage more privileged participants over less privileged ones. And in situations where there is unchecked power over the people being held to account, there may be very little recourse when the consequences of these choices are life threatening, not to mention incongruent with their other needs.

Education, employment, and background checks

Nowhere is an inattention to need clearer, in my reflection, than the enforcement of employment or educational enrollment as a requirement for diversion program compliance. Undoubtedly, somebody wise has written something about personal fulfillment derived from education and employment and why that is essential for personal growth or self-esteem. More important to me is the self determination that comes with even a modicum of financial independence, which is pretty hard to come by without a job for most of us, and literally almost all of us in the diversion program. Education and employment are things I wish more, if not all, people had more access to, particularly high-quality education and dignified well-paid employment. My issue is that use of this as a requirement for program compliance is going to be easier to fulfill for people in a more privileged position than people in a more deprived one.

In my experience, as a relatively privileged person in this particular program, it was certainly easier to enroll in college than to find a job, as I suspect was the case for anyone with access to similar resources. According to economists from the Federal Reserve Bank of St. Louis, in contemporary America, there's a pretty clear sorting mechanism by which family income, academic achievement, and future college enrollment are tightly correlated (Leukhina, 2021). Three of us in the diversion program were in compliance by being enrolled in college as opposed to working, and all of us were doing so as a result of the same meritocratic connections. The two other participants who were complying with program requirements by attending college instead of working, had their parents pick up whatever part of their living expenses weren't covered by financial aid. I had been in a similar situation but had burned through my parents financial goodwill long before this arrest.

Whether it was because they lacked access to the same resources or for some other reason, most of my fellow participants found themselves in a position where if they were going to remain in compliance with the program, they needed to have a job. A proposal easier said than done for people with pending criminal felony charges. Suggesting that having a criminal history creates a barrier to employment by further stigmatizing an already vulnerable population from obtaining something crucial for reducing recidivism, is a frustrating, though not a complicated or even particularly controversial concept. As Griffit, Rade, and Anazodo point out in their 2018 interdisciplinary literature synthesis on the subject, everyone from advocacy nonprofits like the National Employment Law Project and the billionaires David and Charles Koch argue that excluding people with criminal records who are otherwise qualified workers, will harm people seeking employment and organizations by barring access to talented workers (Griffit, Rade and Anazodo, 2019).

While I was enrolled in a diversion program, I knew a few people (and this also applies to myself after finishing college) who were quite literally offered jobs by direct hiring managers, only to have their offers rescinded after a higher-level corporate human resources staff member reviewed the background check. Perhaps the saddest story I have about this was for a man named Adam.

Adam was a middle-aged White man, probably in his late thirties or early forties, who had survived repeated sexual abuse from his father, who at the time of Adam's arrest was still in prison for crimes he had committed against Adam and his younger brother. Adam was enrolled in the diversion program in response to multiple counts of identity theft charges. He had used his grandmother's social security number to illegally to fill oxycontin prescriptions at various pharmacies in the area. By the time I got to know Adam, he had been placed on a special kind of probationary status in the program as it had been around three or four months since he started the program and he had not yet succeeded in starting a job.

Whether this was because (as many participants and court employees suspected) Adam wasn't looking for a job or because he was really struggling, I don't know. But I do know that after Adam was placed on this special probationary status, he began furiously searching for a job. Adam was eventually offered a job at a large chain hardware store, though after he arrived for his first shift, they terminated him when his background check came back showing pending charges for identity theft. These were of course, the very charges for which he was currently in the diversion program to address, but that seemingly was not a negotiable point. Why would it be? This wasn't long after the 2008 recession, a time where over a hundred people had turned out to job fairs to apply for a position like this. With that many applicants, surely there was someone as qualified as Adam who didn't have multiple pending charges, regardless of what the rationale would have been to hire him.

I was in court for my own case on the day they terminated Adam from the program and effectively sentenced him to prison. They took him away in tears while his immediate family watched from the seats. We lost contact after that and I'm sad to say I have no idea where he is today.

The effect background checks has on limiting future employment is, of course, not limited to people active in alternative programs. My codefendant, sentenced to prison instead of to an alternative like me, has only this year, after more than a decade, had the charges removed from his record. Not six months before the removal occurred, he was offered a job that would have been a step up in his current career, only to have the offer rescinded after the letter of employment was sent out as his background check turned up charges related to his arrest.

In response to the lingering effect of background checks on employment, the last decade has seen a rise of legislation and policy that attempts to combat stories like this one, sometimes referred to as "ban the box" (BTB) policies. No doubt the proliferation of stories about difficulties people with a criminal history have in finding a job have contributed to the proliferation of these policies. BTB policies generally refer to any legal change meant to restrict employers access to criminal history information at various points in the hiring process with the goal of preventing otherwise qualified applicants from being screened out. According to the National Employment Law Project, as of 2021, 37 states and over 150 cities and counties had a BTB law of some kind, and more practically, as of the time of the writing 80 percent of the US population now live in a jurisdiction that has "banned the box" laws (Avery and Lu, 2021). Despite the widespread passage of these laws, there is considerable variation among them, with some outright banning criminal background checks in the hiring process, and others banning them at the early stages until later in the process.

Whether or not these laws work as expected is a much more complicated and mostly disappointing story. In a 2021 review of research on BTB laws over the last decade, Stephen Raphael, a University of California Berkeley professor, finds that at best, there is some evidence that these laws have their intended effect of helping people with a criminal record secure employment in the public sector, but there is little benefit in access to private sector jobs (Raphael, 2021). Reaching overall conclusions about these laws, however, is somewhat premature, as many laws vary by jurisdiction, and the extent to which laws that restrict access to all information as compared to those which just delay the information is not well understood (Raphael, 2021).

Perhaps more concerning than whether these laws help people with a record gain employment, is the small but powerful body of research suggesting that in some cases BTBs may have unintended consequences, where employers increase their discrimination against Black job applicants out of a presumption of criminal history when this information is restricted (Raphael, 2021). It is outside the scope of this book to review these consequences in depth. Still, it deserves to be said if there is no way to "ban the box" without this retaliatory effect, advocates and researchers will need to explore other solutions for reducing discrimination in employment against people with criminal history.

BTB law or not, Adam's story demonstrates clearly the potential repercussions of being locked out of the labor market, and his story is one of a million. To consider things from another angle though, rather than elaborating on the ways it's difficult for vulnerable people with limited social resources to find employment with a record, it might be beneficial to see how those with more sources succeed in complying.

***

As I entered my 18th month in the program, having officially aged out of being able to be in compliance by way of higher education, I was faced with the task that nearly everyone else had been faced with—finding a job. Meanwhile, my friend (remember the one from a rich family in the last chapter who had the gun charges dropped), had "succeeded" in finding employment in his father's medical practice, which in reality meant he had reconnected with his father and was on speaking terms and had been given a job illegally working as nurse in his office pulling down a middle-class salary. Me being in a slightly less fortunate situation at the time, applied to three restaurants to be a dishwasher.

My first interview went something like this:

> Yea, cool man, don't worry, about half the folks in the kitchen here are on work release, I'm sure it won't be a problem you're in drug court, why don't you come in Tuesday.
>
> (Anonymous, 2013)

Monday comes around, I call.

> Yea, sorry, man, got a call from a higher up sounds like you didn't pass the background check.
>
> (Anonymous, 2013)

This same outcome was repeated at two more restaurants. When I applied for work at a local Target store I was actually given the offer of employment from the hiring manager, before being told a week later that I'd failed the background check.[17]

Maybe three or 4 weeks after that, I got a full-time job selling tree care door-to-door for just commission and no wage. To his credit, the man who hired me said a lot of nice things about "second chances", and how it was about "the man I was now, not who I'd been", which was refreshing to hear. To supplement the commission-only compensation, I got a part-time gig manually transcribing contact information for people who had recently been in a car accident from the state police public files database (viewable in person only, at the time) to "generate leads" for a chiropractor's office in Seattle.

Tough as it was, what eventually led me to transition out of sales and into an office job, was the recommendation from a family friend for an internship in a public health department. I was qualified for and interested in the internship, but the position was literally not advertised to anyone else, so I was the only applicant. And while this position would ultimately change my life by setting me down the course of a career in policy research, it's only fair to admit that the only reason I got that job was a personal family connection, which at the very least must border on nepotism. Ironically, there were no concerns about criminal background checks for this job, because unlike working retail or in the kitchen of a corporate restaurant, for this position in state government, background checks were not required, or even seemingly even considered to be worth the paperwork.

This is particularly crucial, as at least one study from 2016 suggests that the quality of job someone is able to obtain after release from prison, and perhaps then by extension, after arrest, may be a better predictor of reduced recidivism. Drawing on a study of 1.7 million offenders released from California prisons from 1993 to 2008, Schnepel specifically finds that increased demand for manufacturing and construction jobs particularly, are associated with decreases in recidivism (Schnepel, 2016). This suggests that in addition to whatever options a program can offer a given person for making positive changes in their life, the very real conditions of the quality of jobs available to them influences their prospects. Although not the focus of Schnepel's study, it does seem intuitive then that people who have greater access to employment through preexisting privileges in education or well-connected social networks will likely fare better upon release then people without these.

***

There's one final point that deserves to be reiterated here. Thinking again about Adam's experience looking for a job, and my experience with jobs that didn't require four-year degrees and nepotism, a skeptical reader might wonder, how is it that employers are so easily able to ascertain if someone has an open warrant or pending case against them? After all, don't FBI background checks provide either arrests or convictions, not the date of the next court appearance?

While I have no clear way of knowing if this was directly applicable to me or Adam, it is true that in recent years the use of third-party background checks by employers, covering everything from active and sealed cases to credit and employment history, has become relatively common practice, at least if the FAQs of Indeed.com can be believed (Team, 2021). On top of whatever gains employers get in terms of efficiency or reduced cost of performing background checks if they contract this to a third-party nongovernment provider, it's also worth pointing out that employers also gain legal immunity from any breaches of privacy, defamation, or negligence arising from a third party, which surely must further incentivize some employers to outsource this service (Fair Credit Reporting Act, 2022).

These third-party background check providers often function by using, in addition to public or requested government records, contemporary technology that monitors and extracts vast amounts of publicly available data on individual arrests and jail and court procedures in order to provide this information to interested employers, be these corporations or parents vetting babysitters. This becomes especially concerning considering how much criminal justice data is publicly accessible. I don't know of a comprehensive survey of the US courts, but in nearly every jurisdiction I have ever worked or been arrested, there was a web-based lookup where anyone could find information on who was currently in jail and/or awaiting a court hearing. I've done my own automated data collection of many of these sites to generate statistics related to decarceration, and I think generally a good rule to assume for everyone is: if data is publicly accessible online, it's probably a safe assumption that at some point someone will be able to collect it in mass, using approaches like web scraping.[18]

This means that legal or not, innocent until proven guilty or not, it's very likely that third-party background checks will continue to monitor this type of information. It would be a severe moral hazard to assume that, just because some websites have use agreements prohibit scraping information for use in these background checks, companies who can easily make use of this technology and conceal their behavior through proxies won't continue to do so. This means in practice then, it is very hard to restrict employers from using this information, regardless of whatever seemingly very strict data use laws are put in place.

Perhaps in response to the concern that background checks can be such a hindrance for people after arrest, many states in the US have very strict laws on who can access data about people in the criminal legal system. In some states, requesting structured data on people going through the criminal legal system is severely protected, requiring considerable bureaucratic approval from many different disinterested government employees. Ironically, in many of these same states, the same information about any individual person is still publicly accessible through online web portals, court documents that can be requested, or third-party background checks. Politicians who attempt to enforce or pass very strict data use laws while ignoring what is publicly accessible make sharing data among other government institutions (let alone with outside researchers) more challenging, all the while failing to protect individuals' privacy from third-party checks that leverage these public resources. At best these laws are born of virtue signaling instead of a genuine will to produce effective changes in outcome. At worse they exploit a real desire to protect people's privacy to justify less transparency and to shield the actions and budgets of favored institutions.

There seems to be relatively little interest in auditing third-party background check providers to assess to what extent they comply with state laws or otherwise complicate compliance with diversion programs and other alternatives to incarceration. This is pure speculation, but it seems plausible to me that third-party background checks without oversight may contribute partly to why some BTB laws don't demonstrate positive gains in private sector employment, though it's worth noting that no BTB laws that I'm aware of would have impacted Adam's situation. That is, no BTB laws I know of can prevent revealing pending charge information, even if the pending charge information is clearly related to a program the person is attempting to comply with by looking for a job. If the use of alternatives to incarceration or other diversion programs is going to continue to grow, then we may see an increasing number of people with what appear to be pending charges for sometimes years at a time as a result of their compliance with programs. If we expect people to have any kind of success in obtaining employment from an impersonal employer bound by a corporate policy that mandates denial of employment to anyone with a pending charge, then surely there needs to be a larger conversation on this topic.

Conclusion

If part of the reason we have diversion programs or other alternatives to incarceration is a belief that they can be more effective at reducing future recidivism than incarceration, then it seems intuitive that we would want people at higher risk of future recidivism enrolled in these programs. And yet, if the highest risk people are even considered eligible for these programs, let alone referred to these programs, then compliance is further complicated by what will almost certainly be higher needs, many of which will have raised the person's risk for future offending in the first place.

Thinking back to chapter 1, this presents a complicated path forward for alternative programs looking to combat preexisting disparities and their influence on crime and who is arrested. To recap: through a combination of a lack of financial resources and racial bias, the most deprived people in America are more likely to be targeted for conduct they didn't commit as well as treated more harshly for conduct they did commit. They are more likely to be excluded from reform options on the basis of prior targeting by law enforcement and more likely to have a lack of prosocial connections (such family support or employment) that existed prior to arrest. Then if they manage to still be eligible for a reform program, they face a greater burden to comply with the requirements, because of these very same differences in needs.

To look at things from a different angle, individuals who can afford (or, like the author, whose families can afford) to supplement their own defense or are better positioned to pay for a defense that can redirect them to less punitive outcomes tend to have a further decreased likelihood of reoffending and the benefit of securing a more lenient punishment. These very same people were more likely to have been born and spent their youth somewhere with less police presence and generally had less of a chance of being arrested in the first place. Then, if someone from this type of background is arrested and ultimately offered an alternative program, they will likely have more resources (such as a car, a job, a friend with a spare room, etc.) and will be better positioned to comply with the requirements of alternative programs. This will almost always decrease their chances of reoffending even further, not to mention avoiding things like prison. This, in turn, can have profound consequences for the rest of the person's life, and will certainly influence where they will be decades or more after the start of their interaction with the criminal legal system.

3
Ten years later

Learning objectives

- To gain introductory knowledge of the changes in diversion programs in the United States over the last three decades as well as how treatment of young offenders in these programs varies greatly by birth cohort.
- To gain an introductory understanding of where gaps still persist in who is eligible for alternatives and how they are applied.
- To understand the impact of diversion programs on offenders' lives.

About 10 years ago I turned 20 years old in jail. I was in jail because of a technical violation in the reform program I was attending. Just last year, I turned 30 with a job as a professional researcher and able to support myself and my partner on my own income. By the conventional measure of "success" of any alternative program, I'm doing great; I haven't gone back to jail or prison. Better yet, not only have I not gone back to jail or prison but I'm also much more fulfilled, happier, and stabler in my life than I was 10 years ago. I've left behind cigarettes (mostly) and antidepressants (after talking to a doctor about it), am happily married and we're expecting our first child, and have otherwise lived a satisfyingly rich life for the last 10 years.

To some extent my experience isn't that unique. It's outside the scope of this book to summarize all the research, but in one study from March 2021, researchers assessing the outcome of two Texas-based diversion programs found they reduced recidivism by 50% and increased quarterly employment by 50% (Mueller-Smith and Schnepel, 2020). Another study found that among similarly situated defendants, prison sentencing increases the risk of future offending relative to probation sentencing (Harding et al., 2017). While studies assessing future education and employment success are harder to come by than those measuring recidivism, certainly my own experience is consistent with the first study.

If you believe that harsher punishments deter future behavior it may seem counterintuitive that diversion programs are more effective at reducing recidivism than traditional punishment such as incarceration. However, the findings of the studies noted above are consistent with what experts have identified as the greatest risk factors for criminal and violent behavior. While we can admit there may be something intuitive about the idea that harsher consequences for behavior could disincentive someone from engaging in it, as a broad explanation, it runs the risk of oversimplifying the impulsive way in which some illegal acts occur and the conditions that make this behavior likely in the first place. By removing people from society, placing them into close contact with people with other risky behaviors, and severing their means for legal or higher earning employment, incarceration may exacerbate exactly the conditions that lead to more violent behavior. To put it another way: if dynamic social factors such as meaningful employment, positive mental outlook, and social support system are the sorts of things associated with less offending, surely acknowledging that prison will disrupt all of those in a much more severe way than an alternative or diversion program or probation makes for easy extrapolation.

Changes in drug possession punishment

Not only is my experience of no recidivism after a diversion program not that uncommon, but that I was offered diversion in lieu of prison seems to be part of an increasing trend whereby diversion is becoming a more common option than incarceration, especially for felony drug possession crimes. If I were 10 years older, I have no idea what my life would look like now. This is because the reform program I was referred to would not have existed. In which case, there's an almost guaranteed chance I would have gone to prison instead of being referred to a diversion program. To give just some examples of how that may have changed my life: I almost certainly wouldn't have finished college, which would have ruled out the career I've spent the last seven years in. With a felony on my record, international travel would have been severely restricted, in which case I wouldn't ever have met my partner. More abstractly, the people and experiences that have imbued my life with meaning and me with self-confidence to continue to change my life would have been much further out of reach, so much so that I have no idea how much I'd even resemble the person I am now.

In addition to the changes of my own life's course and likely that of many others as a result of diversion in lieu of prison, the result of deferring more people for drug possession charges from the criminal legal system also means practical changes in the composition of prisons. This has extremely practical ramifications for considering how to reduce mass incarceration in America. To give an example that illustrates this change in the prison composition: The third chapter in one of the most iconic books about mass incarceration in America, Ruth Wilson Gilmore's *Golden Gulag* begins with a quote from a 40-year-old ex-gangster describing his time in prison:

> Last time I was in [prison, in 1992] … More than half the guys, they were in for drugs, for possession. I mean for nothing. That was truly amazing, you know, to me.
>
> (Gilmore, 2007).

Comparing this quote to statistics showing the change in prison populations from the early 1990s to the current date further validates its veracity. Even as prison population rates neared a peak around the time I was arrested in the early 2000s, the proportion of people in prison on drug-related charges was beginning to decline. According to the Bureau of Justice Statistics, drug charges made up 14% of all people in state prisons as of 2019, with drug possession accounting for 4% of that and charges related to drug possession with intent or trafficking charges accounting for 10% (Carson, 2021b). This is down from drug possession accounting to 18% of all people in prison in 2009 (Guerino, Harrison and Sabol, 2011), and 21% in the year 2000 (Beck and Harrison, 2001).[19] Over this same time period state prison incarceration rates rose steadily from 2000 to 2009, from 432 people per 100,000 to 584 people per 100,000, before declining to 477 per 100,000 in 2019 (Carson, 2020).

A lower proportion of the state prison population held on drug charges should not be confused with nobody being held on drug charges. For one, in 2019 the proportion of people held on drug charges in state prisons varied tremendously by state: over a third of all state prisoners in Idaho were held on drug charges, relative to fewer than 4% of all state prisoners in California and Alaska (Carson, 2020). Furthermore, while these aggregate statistics paint a picture of a lower proportion of prisoners incarcerated on drug offenses than reflected in the 1994 quote from Gilmore's book, we shouldn't forget that this varies tremendously by prison facility. It may remain the case that today, 10 years after I was arrested and almost 30 years after the quote from Gilmore's book was authored, there are still thousands of people in prison on any given day on drug possession charges, making up a much larger proportion of federal and minimum security facilities than state medium or higher security ones.

One way to describe these trends in changing responses by the criminal legal system to drug possession is by what Neil and Sampson refer to in their 2021 study as the "birth lottery of history". This study looked at two Chicago-based birth cohorts born between 1976 and 1996, Neil and Sampson looked at cumulative probabilities for lifetime arrest for the two different cohorts. In addition to looking at sociodemographic factors related to deprivation, the authors also look at individual psychosocial factors related to self-control. This means the authors were able to measure a combination of static and dynamic risk factors both seen to have associations with crime and violence depending on how they're measured. What Neil and Sampson observe is remarkable: 70% of individuals born in the mid-1980s were arrested by their mid-twenties as compared to about 25% of those born in the mid-1990s. The changes were most pronounced among people at the lower strata of social advantage, but were also identifiable among those with lower self-control, a critical dynamic risk factor for recidivism or engagement in crime. This latter change was so pronounced that it lead the authors to conclude that:

> Reductions in the chances of arrest have been so large that they have made the low self-control people of one cohort nearly indistinguishable from the high self-control people of a cohort born just one decade earlier.
>
> (Neil and Sampson, 2021, p. 1170)

In a similar study by Shen and colleagues in 2022, researchers explore the extent to which differences in generational risk of arrest, and by extension, the generation of a criminal record, led to differences in the prison population in North Carolina. The authors specifically focus on North Carolina because of a legal change passed in 1994 that created harsh sentencing enhancements for prior criminal history, leading to marked changes in the state's prison population even as crime rates fluctuated (Shen et al., 2020). Shen found that cohorts who experienced the late 1980s and 1990s crime-punishment wave in their young adulthood had a higher probability of being sentenced to prison than the pre-wave cohort, and were given misdemeanor and felony prior convictions in their forties, regardless of offense, offender characteristics, and other factors due primarily to the increased use of their criminal history in sentencing (Shen et al., 2020). Considering the possibilities for bias in arrest, either implicit, racially motivated, or deliberate because of focused resources on higher crime areas, the possibility for scaling disparities in prison populations is not hard to imagine. Consider as well from my own experience how crucial it was that my first arrest did not result in the generation of any criminal history, which fundamentally allowed me to remain eligible for the program I was referred to in lieu of prison.

It is outside the scope of this book to reconcile these studies with the results of the study by Weaver et al. discussed in chapter 1, which suggests that the likelihood of arrest for criminal behavior increased in recent decades, and at much sharper rate for Black youth compare to White youth (Weaver, Papachristos and Zanger-Tishler, 2019). In contrast, Neil and Sampson express skepticism of Weaver use of self-reported data, and fear that may lead to more biased changes in their results. It may also be that Weaver is correct, but that changes in the likelihood of arrest are mediated by alternative responses, or else that Neil and Sampson's focus on one only jurisdiction in a relatively progressive part of the country masks more general changes (Roland and Neil, 2021).

Although it may be challenging to attempt to reconcile these differences, it's important to remember the very real ramifications of this. While my own potential prison sentence would not have lasted more than a few years, others in the same program as me were looking at 5- or even 10-year sentences. Add to this that prison as opposed to treatment may very well increase the risk of recidivism, leading potentially to yet another 5- or 10-year stint in prison once someone was released. And it's clear that for many people incarceration can be an intergenerational experience spanning the entire childhood and adolescence of the children of many people held in a revolving door of incarceration. Difficult as it may be to ascertain if chances of arrest have shifted depending on identical behavior intergenerationally, surely the increased use of reform programs and to some extent decrease in criminal record generation, may feed into some of the shifts in prison populations observed by Shen et al. (2020) in North Carolina.

Gaps in diversion and alternatives to incarceration

While I am obviously biased toward the greater use of diversion and celebrate its increasingly widespread adoption across the United States, there remain some very clear gaps. Directly related to my experience: while there are more than 3,800 drug courts operating throughout the US right now (Office of Justice Programs, 2022), it is simply not the case that everyone who uses drugs is dependent on them, or that all crimes committed are related to drug use (or even selling drugs), however much substance abuse plays a role in criminal offending. For example, not only did my codefendant who went to prison instead of diversion have public representation, but his substance-abuse assessment made it clear he did not have a substance-abuse problem, which suggests that placing him in a drug court program would have been a ridiculous idea. And yet, in our town at least, there were no other alternatives available for him besides incarceration, which only caused more disruption to his life and greater hardship upon release, placing him in some ways in a worse position upon release than when he entered.

If gaps in alternatives exist for someone like my codefendant, they are nowhere near as large as those that exist for people charged with violent crimes or with any violent offenses in their past. As uncomfortable as the idea of alternatives to incarceration for people charged with violent crime may make us, the fact is that people charged with violence or a history of violence make up a larger share of today's prison population, and thus of mass incarceration, than people without violent offenses (Carson, 2021b).

One commonly proposed alternative for some violent crimes is what is often referred to as "restorative justice". As a term, restorative justice has many competing definitions, and as the author of one 2016 article in the journal *Victims & Offenders* points out, there are some who believe it is truly undefinable (Daly, 2016). For a more approachable definition than "undefinable", the Canadian Government refers to restorative justice as "an approach to justice that seeks to repair harm by providing an opportunity for those harmed and those who take responsibility for the harm to communicate about and address their needs in the aftermath of a crime" (Department of Justice Canada, 2021). In my opinion, restorative justice has come to largely refer to any alternative to retributive punishment for a crime of interpersonal victimization. Most often, this refers to various forms of victim and offender mediation, in which victims and offenders are guided through a discussion of the harm caused and reach a consensus for how best to repair the harm, typically with a facilitator from a community-based service providing mediation. This surely does not encompass what is meant by restorative justice for all practitioners of it, and is likely a departure from its original definition, but nevertheless this describes the programs I have seen implemented using the name.

One of the most popular arguments in favor of expanding restorative justice to respond to violence comes from Danielle Sered's 2019 book *Until We Reckon*. Listing heartfelt anecdotes from her program Common Justice, Sered makes a passionate case for expanding the use of programs like these. While there has been some proliferation of restorative justice, particularly for juveniles, for adults this remains a very small fraction of total cases coming into the system. It is Sered's belief that until there exists a response to violence that finds a way to address harms that have existed in the life of a person who committed violence, we are much more likely to see the continuation of a revolving cycle. Summarizing this concisely, Sered states:

> Nearly everyone who has committed harm has survived it, and few have received any formal support to heal. None of the violence people have experienced excuses what they go on to do. But it is unquestionably a factor in why they caused the harm.
>
> (Sered, 2019, p. 120)

It is beyond the scope of this book to give a full description of the many types of restorative justice programs or explain why it is people argue there may or may not be better ways of responding to interpersonal violence as a society. While there is certainly a plethora of interventions labeled as restorative justice with outcomes no doubt as varied as the programs, recent research has identified at least some programs as very successful. However, one of the most high-profile examples of a restorative justice program, San Francisco's Make it Right program, may give us some indication of what it could mean to expand this approach at a larger scale.

The Make it Right program provides restorative justice conferencing for youth ages 13 to 17 who would have otherwise faced relatively serious felony charges for things such as burglary, assault, or motor vehicle theft. Researchers from the California Policy Lab evaluated the program in 2022 using a randomized controlled trial design that is considered the gold standard for developing research related to causal inference. Youth given the opportunity to participate in the program had a 19 percentage points lower likelihood of rearrest within 6 months, which represents a 44% relative reduction to the control group, and these differences persisted for 4 years (Shem-Tov, Raphael and Skog, 2022). Similar reductions were seen in a 2019 study in Utah using a randomized controlled design to look at the use of restorative justice informed treatment along with conventional programs for domestic violence offenders (Mills et al., 2019).

Despite the promising results of programs like Make it Right and other diversion programs or alternatives to incarceration, many people are disqualified from accessing them due to dynamic risk factors like unemployment and homelessness. This is especially true among younger adults, and the reason many programs, such as the Make it Right program, are specifically geared for those under 18. However, individuals who are disqualified based on their dynamic risk factors are often exactly those at the highest risk of reoffending and in need of support to prevent it. According to Latessa et al. in *What Works*, static risk factors such as low family income do not have as significant an impact on recidivism rates as dynamic risk factors like outlook and "criminal thinking" (Latessa, Johnson and Koetzle, 2013). While dynamic risk factors may occur more frequently among those from deprived and unequal backgrounds, failing to offer services to those who need them most based on screening for their greater risk of re-offense can lead to real and tangible differences in who ends up in prison or returns to prison after release.

Talking about recidivism

Whenever an alternative to incarceration, whether that alternative is restorative justice or a drug court, is discussed, it is almost guaranteed that someone will ask something like: "Does participating in the program instead of being incarcerated reduce recidivism?" It's a worthwhile question, even if it's sometimes given too much priority over others. This elicits the questions "what is recidivism?" and/or "what is the best way to measure recidivism?" In my opinion (and it's not a popular one) we should consider recidivism in two ways: one, as the literal act of committing a new illegal behavior; and, two: as a change in a person's responses to their environment that suggest a greater likelihood of engaging in antisocial behavior, and by extension, contact with law enforcement.

Both points we can think of as along a gradient. To the first, it's easy to imagine a large range of illegal behaviors, some of which, such as speeding, or parking violations, are more like petty misbehavior, while others are truly devastating acts of interpersonal violence. To my second point, there are clear changes in dynamic risk factors in a person's behavior and/or psychology, such as becoming increasingly withdrawn and disconnected from prosocial connections, or exhibiting increasingly impulsive decision-making, that indicate regression from what from many treatment resources are designed to address. These behaviors are not in and of themselves illegal or even necessarily harmful acts, but they should be seen as indicators where further intervention, treatment, or other resources could help prevent future harmful behavior. Critically, it's important to understand that far from recidivism being only an aggregate measure of future illegal behavior, these are changes in a person's life that may lead to more serious disruption in their own lives, with potentially devastating loss of stability or life for themselves and others.

If this is an unconventional way of thinking about recidivism, then you might wonder what are more common measurements, and the unfortunate answer is that it varies tremendously across different forms of reporting and studies. As a recent National Academies of Sciences report describes, some studies have relied on self-reported data, while others count any future arrest as recidivism, and still others count only future guilty convictions (National Academies of Sciences, Engineering and Medicine, 2022). Given this vast spectrum of potentially intolerable human behavior, measuring, and worse yet, reconciling many different estimates of recidivism across different studies and government reports, is not a straightforward task. This is hardly a new limitation to point out, as the same National Academies of Sciences report states, that for more than 35 years there have been critiques written about different ways of measuring and talking about recidivism leading to confused interpretations. The report goes on to emphasize problems with the measurement of recidivism that are similar to all problems related to entering the criminal legal system, such as trying to reconcile the bias of who is more likely to be arrested depending on where police resources are focused (National Academies of Sciences, Engineering and Medicine, 2022).

As an example, consider the tradeoffs of measuring recidivism based on self-reported behavior or on administrative data sources. Measuring recidivism with self-reported behavior may do a much better job at capturing unobserved crime that might nevertheless constitute behavior we all wish wouldn't happen. Someone who admits to stealing in a self-reported assessment may never be apprehended for this, but it may signal a regression away from changes they've tried to make in their life after treatment. However, measuring recidivism with self-reported data is of course subject to a person's ability to recall and trust in the reporting system. Try to recall with precise accuracy the number of times you drove over the speed limit in the last 5 to 10 years, and you get the picture of how potentially error prone this system of measurement is for some questions.

In contrast, measuring recidivism using official criminal legal administrative sources, such as the presence of a new arrest for the same person, is guaranteed to be an accurate count within the limitations of whatever database is being used. However, measuring recidivism with administrative data only measures new criminal behavior contingent on, at a minimum, any future contact with the criminal legal system. Consider life in an area with focused deterrence rather than on a university campus, and you get an idea what this might mean in terms of gaps in recording criminal behavior.

These are not merely technicalities to be concerned with. Depending on how recidivism is measured, differences such as using any arrest over any guilty conviction as opposed to any arrest, may show deceptively larger gaps between different populations. For example, compared to the general population, people subjected to considerably more law enforcement supervisions, such as those on probation or parole, may be at far greater risk of any arrest, even for behavior that doesn't lead to a guilty conviction, or only for more minor crimes. The results of this can lead to vastly different assessments of the effectiveness of alternatives to incarceration.

To give examples from my own life as a microcosmic evaluation of treatment's in lieu of prison's effect on recidivism, and measuring my time from graduating the diversion program, I have arguably recidivated, though only in a minor sense and based on self-reported data. I have certainly engaged in illegal traffic behavior at least once in the last 10 years (speeding, parking violations), not to mention the occasional picnic (drinking in public), and even occasional recreational drug use (in New York City? Gasp!). I have not, however, been arrested or even stopped by police for 10 years, and thus none of this behavior has ever been recorded in any kind of administrative database.

Given these limitations, it may be tempting to conclude that recidivism should be thrown out as a measure altogether. However, it is a common critique of reform programs that they increase crime, and critics argue that this is because those who benefit from the programs go on to continue to recidivate in a dangerous way, in other words, commit violent acts against other people that might not have happened had they been incarcerated. Even if it's true that a given program reduces future violent behavior *on average*, to someone who has become the victim of violence from a person who may have otherwise been in jail or prison this surely isn't much consolation. I can think of no easy way to respond to recidivism when it means serious harm to another person, but without taking this consideration seriously, it's hard to imagine the expansion of progressive alternatives to people who made need them the most.

The current mentality among even progressive people working in the criminal legal system for how to talk about recidivism, especially violent or felony recidivism, is a challenging one to counteract. Perhaps to best exemplify this, I once heard from a senior judge:

> When you see on the news that a person out on probation or in a program was just rearrested, every judge, I don't care who you are, thinks two things. One, I hope nobody was hurt, and two, God, I hope he wasn't one of mine.
>
> (Anonymous, 2019)

The same judge went on to say:

> The problem is though, that I could send somebody to prison for 25 years instead, and they might still come out and on the first day kill somebody.
>
> (Anonymous, 2019)

One way to attempt to limit the effect of bias of administrative data on recidivism has been for researchers to focus instead on recidivism only when it involves a felony offense, or only when it involves a crime of interpersonal violence, alleged or otherwise. While this may be an improvement over measuring any type of recidivism, it is still subject to the same limitations, which is why more reflection on this is warranted. There is no easy answer to reconcile this and likely no perfect alternative to punishment that guarantees a person will never hurt another person again.

The willingness of a progressive arm of the criminal legal system to take a risk on my own profile is what led to me being referred to an alternative, but this generosity is clearly not extended to everyone who may benefit from it, nor does it guarantee perfect behavior from then on.

Joel

To illustrate the magnitude of changes in person's life that can accompany the simple measure of recidivism, and the potentially devasting consequences of these changes for themselves and their community, I'll give a short description of one of my fellow diversion participants. On February 21, 2014, I graduated from the diversion program I'd been referred to after my arrest in 2011. That's about a year longer than the program is supposed to take, but some of us are special and have to fail a few UA tests before getting on track. Graduating around the same time as me, and within the time period I should have had I not messed up on the UA, was Joel Nelson, a fellow young man, in his mid to late twenties at the time.

Although we were pretty different people (Joel was athletic, I was in a Dungeons and Dragons campaign and an early adopter of nicotine vapes), demographically we had a lot in common. We both had grown up in an unincorporated part of a midsize rural county, we both had worked on shellfish farms and attended community college, we had the same skin tone (white), were the same gender, and were close in age, not to mention the obvious that we both had ended up in the same diversion program. I wouldn't call us close, but I remember him fondly. He gave me a ride home more than once and I occasionally helped him with his treatment homework. When I saw him speak at a local Recovery Club about his inspirational success story it had been a moving experience for me. I teared up and I (along with many other people) came away idolizing him for his road to change in his life.

I lost touch with Joel after he graduated from the diversion program and didn't think very much about him for almost two years. I gathered from reading future court documents and rumors from mutual friends on social media, that at some point in 2015 or 2016 Joel relapsed. He may have been homeless, and eventually had a warrant out for his arrest (Jackson and Nicholson 2019). I don't know the details of what changed, but it's clear that his life had become more chaotic than it was when he left the program. I often wonder what could have happened, had there been some other way to intervene in Joel's life and connect him back to more services.

On January 5, 2016, Joel Nelson was killed by a sheriff's department deputy, coincidentally the same department that raided my apartment with the narcotics squad back in 2011 (Rosoff, 2016). The official story goes that the deputy was responding to an unrelated call in the area, when he saw a man in his twenties acting suspiciously in a wooded area (Jackson and Nicholson, 2019). The story goes on to say that the deputy confronted Joel, and after talking for a few minutes, Joel then punched the officer in the face, and attempted to take control of the officer's SUV (Jackson and Nicholson, 2019). The deputy attempted to use his taser to subdue Joel, but it was reported to have no effect (Jackson and Nicholson, 2019). Joel then took control of the officer's SUV, and he attempted to drive off with the door on the driver's side open, hitting another vehicle as he drove off and causing minimal damage (Jackson and Nicholson, 2019). At this point the deputy opened fire, striking Joel in the chest and back as he fled in the car. Joel died on the scene shortly thereafter (Jackson and Nicholson, 2019).

There is some dispute about what happened, and this developed into a court case between Joel's family and the sheriff's department. The owner of the property Joel was on when he was stopped by the deputy claims to have heard four shots, including one much earlier (Cloud and Orheim, 2019). The local sheriff had the squad car in which Joel was shot immediately taken for review and cleaning in separate and more conservative counties, prompting skepticism and suspicion of misconduct by some experts in the case (Cloud and Orheim, 2019). The review of the vehicle was conducted by a department managed by the sheriff's brother, and despite claims of photographs taken from inside the car that may have been used for forensic review, the photographs were never produced in court and seemingly could never be located (Cloud and Orheim, 2019). Expert review concluded that after the cleaning of the car, the possibility of review for further evidence was impossible (Cloud and Orheim, 2019). Despite challenges in court from Joel's family and as far as I'm aware, the deputy who shot Joel has not been found guilty of any offenses, nor has the sheriff who presided over the investigation.

I have thought a lot about various other services that could have intervened in Joel's life earlier that may have prevented this situation from happening. Fundamentally, however, Joel is dead because after an altercation with an officer, the officer elected to use lethal force while Joel attempted to flee. Had the officer been able to de-escalate the situation, or let Joel flee while waiting for his backup to arrive, Joel would be alive. Instead, he left behind a fiancée and a father who has now lost both his sons.

Sadly, many other people who've attempted to flee police share Joel's experience. Analysis of Mapping Police Violence data in a recent *Guardian* article shows that from 2015 to July 16, 2022 nearly one-third of people killed by police were "running away, driving off, or attempting to flee when the officer fatally shot or used lethal force against them" (Mahdawi, 2022). If we think back to Andre and Bryson's encounter with police, in the same town where Joel was shot, they too were shot while attempting to flee after an altercation with an officer.

Mental illness and police violence

Although I do not know if this was relevant to Joel's situation, it's worth noting too that people with mental illness may be at far greater risk of police violence. A 2015 advocacy report claims that 1 in 50 adults has untreated severe mental illness, but about 1 in 4 fatal police shootings involves a person showing signs of untreated severe mental illness (Fuller et al., 2015). However, as the same report elaborates, data are severely limited, with very limited official reporting making precise validation of these numbers challenging and leading the officers to rely on databases based on aggregations of media stories (Fuller et al., 2015). One such database, Mapping Police Violence, cited often throughout this book, shows that 23% of deaths from police violence in 2022 were against people showing signs of mental illness (Mapping Police Violence, 2023).[20]

In addition to experiencing violence, there is some evidence that people with severe mental illness are more likely to have a fatal encounter with the police. This may be due primarily to differences in police behavior during confrontations with someone with severe mental illness. Two studies using officer self-reported data suggest that police are more likely to use force against people with serious mental illness, but this effect dissipates when factors related to resistance to arrest are accounted for (Johnson, 2011; Mulvey and White, 2014). One more recent study, using empirical data from eight police agencies, finds a weak effect, suggesting police are more likely to use violence even accounting for these factors, though not by much (Rossler and Terrill, 2016). The same study finds that injury or death is more common, but after controlling for differences in resistance and violence against the police officer, there is no statistically significant difference (Rossler and Terrill, 2016). Additionally, a 2016 white paper published by the Ruderman Family Foundation argues that people with other types of disabilities beyond mental illness, may also be at increased risk of violent interactions with law enforcement, though precise estimates are hard to define (Perry and Carter-Long, 2016).

Given the above, advocates of reform tend to argue that this is a perfect example of why police are not the best people to respond to people showing signs of untreated mental illness. The argument is that officers who are trained to specifically respond with force to certain types of resistance or violent behavior, and who represent a tacit threat of arrest and incarceration, may escalate situations further to the point where force is used. Alternatively, it's suggested that people trained in de-escalation techniques, and more familiar with how to respond to mental illness, may be better at responding to crises like these without the use of lethal force or other violence.

Regardless of whether differences in resisting arrest account for differences in being a victim of violence by the police, the evidence suggests that having a mental illness increases the risk of a police encounter, and this can quickly turn violent. These violent consequences are part of what I mean when I say that recidivism doesn't necessarily mean an aggregated count of illegal behavior, but can be a signal for a dramatic shift in a person's life, where the possibility of future law enforcement interaction could bring about its end. Whatever happened with the changes in Joel's life, the consequences were devastating. His recovery story had inspired a community, and he had been a loving partner and fiancé. If something could have intervened in his life earlier and help reconnect him to recovery, perhaps he never would've been in the situation he was in the first place. Perhaps if someone other than a sheriff's deputy, or the deputy himself, had been able to de-escalate the situation, Joel would still be alive. This is what's at stake when we talk about alternatives attempting to help people change their lives, whether that's in terms of their own future behavior or the actions of a violent legal system.

Conclusion

I read the news about Joel the day after it happened, in an outdoor café in Tasmania, Australia, where I had been working in a food truck, about as far as I could humanly get from where I was born without having to learn to speak another language. On the continuum of how much of American popular culture cared about police killings of unarmed people, this was a moment far from mainstream interest, but careening toward more popular coverage such as would be seen around 2020. Stories about Eric Garner and Sandra Bland were still in the news, Black Lives Matters protests made headlines, but we were still a hell of a long way from the mainstreaming effects the George Floyd protests in 2020 would have on conversations about police violence in America. Consequently, there was almost no media coverage of Joel's death, and what did exist seemed to mostly focus on reminding the audience that the deputy involved was a veteran of the police and military with 20 years of experience. While more similar stories have made headlines in recent years, at the time of Joel's death, media coverage was scarce and unless someone was an immediate family member, friend, or as in my case, a fellow diversion graduate, there would be very little reason to notice.

Some years after Joel's death the events gained more coverage, in no small part thanks to the work of organizers with the Seattle-based Not This Time, an organization started by Andre Taylor after his brother Che Taylor was shot and killed by police. Joel's partner and father joined the organization, and were present for the signing of legislation that resulted in changes to Washington state law to mandate de-escalation training for police officers and make it easier to prosecute police who improperly use lethal force[21] (Justice for Joel Nelson, 2021).

My life today, indeed my ability to be writing this book right now, seems to me to be as much a product of reforms that connected me with treatment services in lieu of prison 10 years ago, as much as it is a product of my demographics and socioeconomic status. There are many people who are not this lucky, who by accident of birth were not living in a jurisdiction in the United States that would have offered the type of reformed treatment program I received. There are many more still, who were offered the exact program, and who did not succeed, often because their needs were much higher, often in a way that tracks with socioeconomic status. Progressive reforms like those I've benefited from can be life-changing for some people, and that alone makes them worth supporting. However, at least in my own experience, it seems to me that those who are offered alternatives, and those who succeed in them, will tend toward being more socially privileged, and will fall along the same gradient of people who are less likely to be criminal offenders and victims of crime.

It's as though through progressive reform to the criminal justice system, we're constantly redrawing a circle around a pool of the least vulnerable people, in a crowd of extremely vulnerable people, who have been caught doing something harmful or unacceptable, in order to declare that these are people whom society has declared would be better off if we addressed their problematic behavior with services intended to change the conditions of their lives. While expanding the circle of protection has benefits, so too does shrinking the pool of vulnerable people in the first place. Otherwise, it is as though the most vulnerable people, mostly by being unlucky in terms of socioeconomic status of their families, are left in the worst-case scenario, permanently stuck outside of attempts to address their harmful behavior with services intended to change the circumstances that produce that behavior.

Suggested assignments and projects

Research paper

Ask students to select a topic introduced in this book and prepare a short research paper that elaborates on their selection. This could take a variety of forms, though the author suggests a more productive one may be structuring the paper as a policy paper, where a chosen topic is described as a problem, and students review and propose potential solutions. For example, in chapter 1, the author contrasted wage theft with retail theft, giving a characterization that suggests retail theft may be a comparatively less harmful behavior based on the estimated loss in annual wages to victims of wage theft as opposed to the effect on net profits for retail stores. Wage theft, however, is much less likely to be prosecuted and is often not a part of the rhetoric about crime. Students may decide to dig deeper into research on this topic, and propose and/or review recommendations that discuss either wage theft, or alternatives to current approaches to retail theft.

Alternatively, students may be interested in a more exploratory topic, for example, the proliferation of different types of alternatives to incarceration or diversion programs. Students could write a summary research paper that describes other types of alternatives and how they've emerged over the past several decades in the US criminal legal system, without necessarily formulating a problem statement or researching and proposing solutions.

Reflection paper

A large portion of this book centers on the personal experiences of the author and the contrasts to the experiences of those around him. Assigning students to write a short paper in which they reflect on feelings or memories the book prompted for them or from their own experiences, may be a useful way to prompt a more thoughtful synthesis of the material.

Current events analysis

Assign students to follow current news articles and/or social media discussions about a criminal justice reform or to critique a reform that is currently dominating the headlines. Ask students to consider ways in which preexisting social inequalities are either discussed or omitted from these contemporary conversations, drawing parallels to examples from the text. Students could prepare a summary of this as either a short paper or presentation.

Notes

1. I haven't done an exhaustive review of the literature, but certainly plenty of research on adverse childhood experiences has found an association with substance use disorders later in life, and to some extent criminal behavior, as measured by arrest and conviction. For more information see Leza et al. (2021), Douglas et al. (2010) and Reavis et al. (2013).

2. I'm not an expert in this area, but some research, where particularly young adults are unlikely to complete treatment and those that do not complete treatment continue heavy substance abuse, backs up his point. Whether that necessarily extrapolates to future treatment referrals or arrest may be another question, though it was certainly the case for me. For more information see Pettinati et al. (1996), Tate et al. (2011) and Krawczyk et al. (2021).

3. Interestingly, from about 2010 until 2020, this trend shifted in a different direction. As of 2020, Washington state's overdose death rate per 100,000 residents was close to 30% lower than the national average (Kaiser Family Foundation, 2023). At the risk of overstepping my expertise, I can't help but imagine that this has more to do with a progressive stance on Narcan and harm reduction than it has to do with decreased opioid use in Washington state. This deduction is based on observation of the number of discarded needles you can still count walking down the main strip of my hometown.

4. You can Google the term "cop knock" for a free sound effect if you have to, but if you know it, you know it.

5. Author's own analysis of data through media interviews with medical websites like WebMD and therapy.com. These are not comprehensive sources, but anecdotally, they do match what I recall from the time.

6. According to media round ups for the tenth anniversary of Trayvon Martin's death in 2022, this was a galvanizing moment for many people, myself included (Baldwin, 2022; Jackson, Bailey, and Welles, 2020; Munro, 2012; Reis, 2022).

7. For those who don't know, Jussie Smollett is a Black and gay actor who at the time had a successful role in a TV drama called *Empire*. He was notoriously sentenced to jail in Chicago for reporting a fake hate crime incident (Gonzales and Dwyer, 2019; Jacobs and Chiarito, 2022).

8. "Similarly situated" means here and in the rest of the text, fitting a statistical model that controls for criminal history and type of charges filed.

9. There is no consensus among researchers studying police stops on the relevant population size required to generate population rates for traffic stops in a given area. As intuitive as census level populations might be as a starting point, considering what's known about undercounts of Native American, Black, and other people of color relative to White people, there is reason to suspect this could artificially depress counts. Maybe more importantly, it's true that many people commute every day to places they don't live in, and are thus at risk of a police stop in transit. Furthermore, the use of police stop data to assess this question remains complicated by unknown data-quality issues. For example, our own analysis of the Stanford Open Policing Project data for Pierce County, Washington, where we worked, found Native American to be much less likely than White people to be stopped by the police. In contrast, checking state patrol data from the same source for the states Arizona and Montana, who have some of the largest Native American populations and usable data, finds Native American people much more likely to be stopped in Arizona, and less in Montana. More work is needed to understand the quality of tracking in this data before we can rely on it for analysis. For more see Braunstein (2017).

10. Author's analysis of data available from Mapping Police Violence as of July 2022 (Mapping Police Violence, 2022b).

A more robust analysis, albeit with a smaller sample of data, was found in (DeGue, Fowler, and Calkins, 2016).

11. Author's analysis of data available from Mapping Police Violence as of July 2022 (Mapping Police Violence, 2022b). Note that Oregon indicates no deaths by Native Americans, but it's unclear to what extent this is related to limited data, and I suspect this is a data quality problem.

12. Author's analysis of geocoded Mapping Police Violence data, 2013–2022 and US census total populations of reservations estimated at 1,664,107 people for 2020 as compared to the total US population reported in 2020, range of estimates reflects a highly imprecise measure of counting only the total reservation population to roughly twice as much assumed to be within ten miles. Data drawn from Mapping Police Violence with US census population estimates from the American Community Survey and Mapping Police Violence (Mapping Police Violence, 2022b; United States Census Bureau, 2023).

13. For examples of a few studies from Suffolk County, Massachusetts, and Chicago, Illinois, see papers from Flingai et al. (2022) and Levin (2022).

14. Figure 2 above the ratio of prison admissions among Black and White non-Hispanic people ages to 15–64 in 2016, contrasted against the ratio of percent of people living below the federal poverty level. Demographic data were collected from the American Community Survey Five Year Estimates (2012–2016) while prison admission data come from the Vera Institute's curated BJS data on incarceration trends (Vera Institute of Justice, 2023). Counties with no prison or census data were omitted, and San Francisco County, CA, as outlier with a Black/White prison admission rate ratio of 40.9 and poverty ratio of 3.9 was omitted from the chart for clarity, for a total of 53 out of 63 urban counties in America represented in Figure 2.

15. Simple assault typically refers to a type of interpersonal violence without injury, or in some cases physical contact, and may include verbal assaults or threats. It is often a

misdemeanor offense and is generally thought to be much more common than physical violence.

16. Reporting from the journalist Sam Dean at the *Los Angeles Times* suggests that the Retail Industry Leaders Association estimate is based on only five reported estimates from major retailers and in turn used to estimate total losses (Dean, 2021). Dean reports that this reliance on such a small sample is met with heavy skepticism by analysts at the National Retail Federation, a much longer standing organization (Dean, 2021). If this $68 billion figure is correct, then a crude estimate suggests retail theft accounts for closer to 2% of profits from sales rather than 0.07%.

17. I was later distantly part of a class action lawsuit against Target for this policy (Campbell, 2017). I got a grand total of around $15 from this, feasibly the cost of the job application and the background check fee.

18. "Web scraping" is a way of automatically gathering data from websites. It can involve different techniques, ranging from highly sophisticated custom programming to free browser plug-ins. The goal is to collect, record, or extract the data in a more efficient way. At scale, it can allow for simultaneously collecting data from thousands of websites on an automated basis.

19. For comparing proportions from 2009 to the year 2000, see table 16 in the report by (Beck, 2001) and note there may be a methodological difference here from the last two reports cited above.

20. This proportion is based on the author's own analysis of Mapping Police Violence data as of May 2023, relying on the assessment of staff from Mapping Police Violence's whether the article indicated the victim showed signs of mental illness. For more detail on how this was determined, refer to the Mapping Police Violence methodology (Mapping Police Violence, 2022a).

21. Joel's family continues the fight and plans to appeal the case against the officer involved.

References

Agan, A., Doleac, J. and Harvey, A. (2022). Misdemeanor Prosecution. *Working Paper 28600,* August. Washington, DC: National Bureau of Economic Research. DOI: 10.3386/w28600

Aisch, G., Buchanan, L., Cox, A. and Quealy, K. (2017). Some Colleges Have More Students from the Top 1 Percent than the Bottom 60. Find Yours. 18 January. *The New York Times*. [Online]. Available at: www.nytimes.com/interactive/2017/01/18/upshot/some-colleges-have-more-students-from-the-top-1-percent-than-the-bottom-60.html [Accessed Oct. 2023].

Alexander, M. (2010). *The New Jim Crow: Mass Incarceration in the Age of Colorblindness*. New York City: The New Press.

Alliance for Safety and Justice. (2016). *Crime Survivors Speak: The First-Ever National Survey of Victims' Views on Safety and Justice*. Oakland, CA: Alliance for Safety and Justice.

Anonymous. (2010a). Personal communication [Conversation with a White undergraduate student].

Anonymous. (2010b). Personal communication [Conversation with a diversion program staff member].

Anonymous. (2011a). Personal communication [Conversation with a private defense attorney].

Anonymous. (2011b). Personal communication [Conversation with a diversion program staff member].

Anonymous. (2011c). Personal communication [Conversation with a college professor].

Anonymous. (2012). Personal communication [Conversation with a narcotics anonymous sponsor].

Anonymous. (2013). Personal communication [Conversation with restaurant hiring manager].

Anonymous. (2019). Personal communication [Conversation with a senior criminal court judge].

ATTOM. (2022). U.S. Foreclosure Activity Drops to an All-Time Low in 2021. [Online]. Available at: www.attomdata.com/news/market-trends/foreclosures/attom-year-end-2021-u-s-foreclosure-market-report/ [Accessed Jan. 2023].

Avery, B. and Lu, H. (2021). *Ban the Box: U.S Cities, Counties, and States Adopt Fair Hiring Policies*. New York City: National Employment Law Project.

Baglivio, M. T., Epps, N., Swartz, K., Huq, M. S., Sheer, A. and Hardt, N. S. (2014). The Prevalence of Adverse Childhood Experiences (ACS) in the Lives of Juvenile Offenders. *Journal of Juvenile Justice*, 3, pp. 1–23.

Baldwin, R. (2022). Trayvon Martin's Killing 10 Years Ago Changed the Tenor of Democracy. 26 February. NPR. [Online]. Available at: www.npr.org/2022/02/26/1083233572/trayvon-martin-black-lives-matter [Accessed Oct. 2023].

Baran, H. and Campbell, E. (2021). *Forced Arbitration Helped Employers Who Committed Wage Theft Pocket $9.2 Billion in 2019 From Workers in Low-Paid Jobs*. New York City: National Employment Law Project.

Beck, A. J. and Harrison, P. M. (2001). *Prisoners in 2000*. Washington, DC: Bureau of Justice Statistics.

Bhutta, N., Chang, A. C., Dettling, L. J., Hsu, J. W. and Hewitt, J. (2020). Disparities in Wealth by Race and Ethnicity in the 2019 Survey of Consumer Finances. *FEDS Notes*. [Online]. Available at: www.federalreserve.gov/econres/notes/feds-notes/disparities-in-wealth-by-race-and-ethnicity-in-the-2019-survey-of-consumer-finances-20200928.html [Accessed Oct. 2023].

Braga, A. A., Weisburd, D. and Turchan, B. (2019). Focused Deterrence Strategies Effects on Crime: A Systematic Review. *Campbell Systematic Reviews*, 9 September, 15(3), p. e1051.

Braunstein, R. (2017). Case Studies in the Development of Reliable and Valid Social Problems Source Data. *Great Plains Sociologist*, 27(1).

Brown, C. (2019). Incarceration and Earnings: Distributional and Long-Term Effects. *Journal of Labor Research*, 40, pp. 58–83.

Campbell, L. (2017). *$8.5M Settlement Reached in Target Background Check Class Action Lawsuit*. Santa Cruz, CA: Lawyers and Settlements.

Capitol Hill Seattle. (2011). Round up | What's Wrong with the Seattle Police Department? – Update: DOJ Report. 19 December.

Carson, A. E. (2020). *Prisoners in 2019*. Washington, DC: Bureau of Justice Statistics.

Carson, A. E. (2021a). *Mortality in Local Jails, 2000–2019 – Statistical Tables*. Washington, DC: Bureau of Justice Statistics.

Carson, A. E. (2021b). *Prisoners in 2020 – Statistical Tables*. Washington, DC: Bureau of Justice Statistics.

Carter, M. (2015). Calm Urged as Olympia Investigates Police Shootings of 2 Men. *The Seattle Times*. [Online]. Available at: www.seattletimes.com/seattle-news/law-justice/calm-urged-as-olympia-investigates-shootings-of-2-men/ [Accessed May 2023].

Centre for Analytic Criminology. (2023). Situational Action Theory (SAT). University of Cambridge. [Online]. Available at: www.cac.crim.cam.ac.uk/resou/sat [Accessed Oct. 2023].

Cloud, D. R. and Orheim, A. (2019). Brief of Appellee Joseph A. Nelson in Joseph A. Nelson v. Thurston County, et al. Westlaw, 2019, WL 5964932 (C.A.9).

Cohen, T. H. and Reaves, B. A. (2007). *Pretrial Release of Felony Defendants in State Courts*. s.l.: Bureau of Justice Statistics.

Color of Change, ACLU Campaign for Smart Justice. (2017). *Selling Off Our Freedom*. s.l.: Color of Change, ACLU Campaign for Smart Justice.

Cooper, D. and Kroeger, T. (2017). *Employers Steal Billions from Workers' Paychecks each Year*. Seattle, WA: The Economic Policy Institute.

Council for Court Excellence, The National Reentry Network for Returning Citizens, and Vera Institute of Justice. (2019). *Jails & Justice: A Framework for Change*. Washington, DC: Council for Court Excellence.

Daly, K. (2016). *What is Restorative Justice? Fresh Answers to a Vexed Question*. Victims & Offenders, 11(1). https://doi.org/10.1080/15564886.2015.1107797

Dawson, P. (2022). *Punishment. Public Lectures and Events*. Houghton: The London School of Economics. [Online]. Available at: www.lse.ac.uk/lse-player?id=dd0ad338-d6cf-4009-8f60-a5f7e3268fe6

Dean, S. (2021). Retailers Say Thefts Are at Crisis Level. The Numbers Say Otherwise. *Los Angeles Times*. [Online]. Available at: www.latimes.com/business/story/2021-12-15/organized-retail-theft-crime-rate [Accessed Oct. 2023].

DeGue, S., Fowler, K. A. and Calkins, C. (2016). Deaths Due to Use of Lethal Force by Law Enforcement. *American Journal of Preventive Medicine*, November, 51(5), pp. S173–S187.

Department of Justice Canada. (2021). Restorative Justice. [Online]. Available at: www.justice.gc.ca/eng/cj-jp/rj-jr/index.html [Accessed Oct. 2023].

Deshpande, M. and Mueller-Smith, M. (2022). Does Welfare Prevent Crime? The Criminal Justice Outcomes of Youth Removed from SSI. *Quarterly Journal of Economics*, 137(4), pp. 2263–2307. https://doi.org/10.1093/qje/qjac017

Douglas, K. R., Chan, G., Gelernter, J., Arias, A. J., Anton, R. F., Weiss, R. D., Brady, K., Poling, J., Farrer, L. and Kranzlera, H. R. (2010). Adverse Childhood Events as Risk Factors for Substance Dependence: Partial Mediation by Mood and Anxiety Disorders. *Addiction Behavior*, 35(1), pp. 7–13.

Dunn, K., Munoz, M. and Taylor, A. (2018). *Examining Disparities and Implicit Bias in the Prosecution of Misdemeanors in Tacoma Municipal Court*. Seattle, WA: University of Washington.

Fair Credit Reporting Act. (2022). 15 U.S.C. § 1681. [Online]. Available at: www.ftc.gov/system/files/ftc_gov/pdf/545A-FCRA-08-2022-508.pdf [Accessed Oct. 2023].

Fajnzylber, P., Lederman, D. and Loayza, N. (2002). What Causes Violent Crime? *European Economic Review*, 46(7), pp. 1323–1357.

Federal Reserve System. (2016). *Survey of Consumer Finances*. Washington, DC: Board of Governors of the Federal Reserve System.

Flingai, S., Sahaf, M., Battle, N. and Castaneda, S. (2022). *An Analysis of Racial Disparities in Police Traffic Stops in Suffolk County, Massachusetts, from 2010 to 2019*. Brooklyn: The Vera Institute of Justice.

Fuller, D. A., Lamb, R. H., Biasotti, M. and Snook, J. (2015). Overlooked in the Undercounted: The Role of Mental Illness in Fatal Law Enforcement Encounters. Treatment Advocacy Center. [Online]. Available at: www.treatmentadvocacycenter.org/storage/documents/overlooked-in-the-undercounted.pdf [Accessed Oct. 2023].

Gilmore, R. W. (2007). *Golden Gulag: Prisons, Surplus, Crisis, and Opposition in Globalizing California*. Oakland, CA: University of California Press.

Gonzales, R. and Dwyer, C. (2019). 'Empire' Actor Jussie Smollett Arrested on Charges of Filing False Police Report. *NPR*. 20 February.

Gordon, G. , Jones, J. B. , Neelakantan, U. and Athreya, K. B. (2021). Incarceration, Earnings and Race. *FRB Richmond Working Paper No. 21-11*, 1 July.

Griffit, J. N., Rade, C. B. and Anazodo, K. S. (2019). Criminal History and Employment: An Interdisciplinary Literature Synthesis. *Equality, Diversity, and Inclusion*, 38(5), pp. 505–528.

Gross, S. R., Possley, M., Otterbourg, K., Stephens, K., Paredes, J. W. and O'Brien, B. (2022). *Race and Wrongful Convictions in the United States*. s.l.: National Registry of Exonerations.

Guerino, P., Harrison, P. M. and Sabol, W. J. (2011). *Prisoners in 2010*. Washington, DC: Bureau of Justice Statistics.

Hansen, E. (2017). The Forgotten Minority in Police Shootings. 13 November. CNN. [Online]. Available at: https://edition.cnn.com/2017/11/10/us/native-lives-matter/index.html [Accessed Oct. 2023].

Harding, D. J., Morenoff, J. D., Nguyen, A. P. and Bushway, S. D. (2017). Short- and Long-Term Effects of Imprisonment on Future Felony Convictions and Prison Admissions. *Proceedings of the National Academy of Sciences of the United States of America*, 2 October, 114(42), pp. 11103–11108.

Jackson, G. E. and Nicholson, J. R. (2019). Reply Brief of Defendant-Appellant John D. Snaza in Joseph A. Nelson v. Thurston County, et al. Westlaw, 2019, WL 6529582 (C.A.9).

Jackson, S. J., Bailey, M. and Welles, B. F. (2020). Trayvon Martin and the Hashtag Campaign That Set the Stage for Black Lives Matter. 5 June. The MIT Press Reader. [Online]. Available at: https://theader.mitpress.mit.edu/trayvon-martin-hashtag-black-lives-matter-movement/ [Accessed Oct. 2023].

Jacobs, J. and Chiarito, R. (2022). Jussie Smollett Sentenced to Jail for False Report of a Hate Crime. 10 March. *The New York Times*. [Online]. Available at: www.nytimes.com/2022/03/10/arts/television/jussie-smollett-sentencing.html [Accessed Oct. 2023].

Jez, S. J. (2008). The Influence of Wealth and Race in Four-Year College Attendance. *Research & Occasional Paper Series: CSHE.* Berkeley, CA: CSHE.

Johnson, R. R. (2011). Suspect Mental Disorder and Police Use of Force. *Criminal Justice and Behavior*, 38(2). [Online]. Available at: https://doi.org/10.1177/0093854810388160

Justice for Joel Nelson. (2021). Facebook. s.l.: s.n. [Online]. Available at: www.facebook.com/Justiceforjoelnelson/?ref=page_internal&locale=ms_MY&paipv=0&eav=AfajsbKiQ24QBV3tc_NSNkG9pyRYJocE4uRhqJPwnXb1rcNd3uPT3fHz6lJ7mqvZBOk

Kaiser Family Foundation. (2023). Drug Overdose Death Rate (per 100,000 Population). [Online]. Available at: www.kff.org/other/state-indicator/drug-overdose-death-rate-per-100000-population/?activeTab=graph&currentTimeframe=0&startTimeframe=21&selectedDistributions=drug-overdose-deaths&selectedRows=%7B%22states%22:%7B%22oregon%22:%7B%7D,%22washington%22 [Accessed Jan. 2023].

Kanu, H. (2021). Minneapolis' Rejection of a New Kind of Policing is About Politics, Not Policy. Reuters. [Online]. Available at: www.reuters.com/legal/government/minneapolis-rejection-new-kind-policing-is-about-politics-not-policy-2021-11-05/ [Accessed Oct. 2023].

Krawczyk, N., Williams, A. R., Saloner, B. and Cerdá, M. (2021). Who Stays in Medication Treatment for Opioid Use Disorder? A National Study of Outpatient Specialty Treatment Settings. *Journal of Substance Use & Addiction Treatment*, 126. DOI: 10.1016/j.jsat.2021.108329.

Latessa, E. J., Johnson, S. L. and Koetzle, D. (2013). *What Works (and Doesn't) in Reducing Recidivism.* 1st ed. s.l.: Routledge.

Leslie, E. and Pope, N. G. (2017). The Unintended Impact of Pretrial Detention on Case Outcomes: Evidence from New York City Arraignments. *The Journal of Law and Economics,* 60(3), pp. 529–557.

Leukhina, O. (2021). *Meritocracy in College Admissions* [Interview]. 30 June.

Levin, J. (2022). *Racially Disproportionate Traffic Stops Do Not Make Chicago Neighborhoods Safer*. s.l.: ACLU Illinois.

Leza, L., Siria, S., López-Goñi, J. J. and Fernández-Montalvo, J. (2021). Adverse Childhood Experiences (ACEs) and Substance Use Disorder (SUD): A Scoping Review. *Drug and Alcohol Dependence*, 221. https://doi.org/10.1016/j.drugalcdep.2021.108563

Light, M. T. and Ulmer, J. T. (2016). Explaining the Gaps in White, Black, and Hispanic Violence since 1990: Accounting for Immigration, Incarceration, and Inequality. *American Sociological Review*, 81(2), pp. 290–315.

Liu, P., Nunn, R. and Shambaugh, J. (2018). *The Economics of Bail and Pretrial Detention*. s.l.: The Hamilton Project.

Looney, A. and Turner, N. (2018). *Work and Opportunity before and after Incarceration*. Washington, DC: The Brookings Institution.

Luminosity, University of Chicago Crime Lab New York. (2020). *Updating the New York City Criminal Justice Agency Release Assessment*. New York: New York Criminal Justice Agency.

MacDonald Hoauge & Bayless (2018). Police Killing of Native Woodcarver Results in $1.5 Million Civil Rights Settlement and Changes to Seattle Police Department. [Online]. Available at: www.mhb.com/cases/police-killing-of-native-woodcarver-resu lts-in-15-million-civil-rights-settlement-and-changes-to-seattle-police-department [Accessed Oct. 2023].

Mahdawi, A. (2022). 'Hunted': One in Three People Killed by US Police Were Fleeing, Data Reveals. *The Guardian*. [Online]. Available at: www.theguardian.com/us-news/2022/jul/28/hun ted-one-in-three-people-killed-by-us-police-were-fleeing-data-reveals [Accessed Oct. 2023].

Mapping Police Violence. Campaign Zero. (2022a). Mapping Police Violence: Data & Methodology. [Online]. Available at:

https://mappingpoliceviolence.org/files/MappingPoliceViole nce_Methodology.pdf [Accessed Oct. 2023].

Mapping Police Violence. Campaign Zero. (2022b). Mapping Police Violence. 30 November. [Online]. Available at: https:// mappingpoliceviolence.org/ [Accessed Oct. 2023].

Mapping Police Violence. Campaign Zero. (2023). Mapping Police Violence. 23 May. [Online]. Available at: https://mappingpolicev iolence.org/ [Accessed Oct. 2023].

Mariner, J. (2001). *No Escape: Male Rape in U.S. Prisons*. s.l.: Human Rights Watch.

McCann, A. (2022). *State Economies with the Most Racial Equality*. s.l.: WalletHub.

Mills, L. G., Barocas, B., Butters, R. P. and Ariel, B. (2019). A Randomized Controlled Trial of Restorative Justice-Informed Treatment for Domestic Violence Crimes. *Nature Human Behaviour*, 3, pp. 1284–1294.

Mok, P. L. H., Antonsen, S., Pedersen, C. B., Carr, M. J., Kapur, N., Nazroo, J. and Webb, R. T. (2018). Family Income Inequalities and Trajectories through Childhood and Self-Harm and Violence in Young Adults: A Population-Based, Nested Case-Control Study. *Lancet Public Health*, 3, pp. e498–507.

Monarrez, T. and Washington, K. (2020). *Racial and Ethnic Representation in Postsecondary Education*. Washington, DC: Urban Institute: Center on Education Data and Policy.

Movement for Black Lives. (2016a). Policy Platforms. [Online]. Available at: https://m4bl.org/policy-platforms/ [Accessed Jan. 2023].

Movement for Black Lives. (2016b). Restructure Tax Codes. [Online]. Available at: https://m4bl.org/policy-platforms/restruct ure-tax-codes/ [Accessed Jan. 2023].

Mueller-Smith, M. and Schnepel, K. T. (2020). Diversion in the Criminal Justice System. *The Review of Economic Studies*, 24 July, 88(2), pp. 883–936.

Mulvey, P. and White, M. (2014). The Potential for Violence in Arrests of Persons with Mental Illness. *Policing: An International Journal*. 37(2). https://doi.org/10.1108/PIJPSM-07-2013-0076

Munro, A. (2012). Shooting of Trayvon Martin. 26 February. Britannica. [Online]. Available at: www.britannica.com/event/shooting-of-Trayvon-Martin [Accessed Oct. 2023].

Napoleon, V. (2022). *Remaking Justice: From Incremental Reforms to Real Accountability*. Lisbon: Law and Society Association.

National Academies of Sciences, Engineering, and Medicine. (2022). *The Limits of Recidivism: Measuring Success after Prison*. Washington, DC: That National Academies Press.

National Institute of Justice. (2014). *From Youth Justice Involvement to Young Adult Offending*. Washington, DC: Department of Justice.

National Retail Federation. (2021). Organized Retail Crime Remains a Growing Threat. [Online]. Available at: https://web.archive.org/web/20230710220848/https://cdn.nrf.com/sites/default/files/2018-10/NRF-NRSS-Industry-Research-Survey-2018.pdf [Accessed Jan. 2023].

Neil, R. and Sampson, R. J. (2021). The Birth Lottery of History: Arrest over the Life Course of Multiple Cohorts Coming of Age, 1995–2018. *American Journal of Sociology*, 126(5), pp. 1127–1178.

New York (City), City Magistrates' Court. (1962). *Manhattan Bail Project: Official Court Transcripts, October 1961-June 1962*. New York City: Vera Institute of Justice.

New, J. (2015). What Happens on Campus Stays on Campus? Inside Higher Ed. [Online]. Available at: www.insidehighered.com/news/2015/02/27/how-institutions-handle-drug-violations-varies-greatly [Accessed Oct. 2023].

Nowotny, K. M., Rogers, R. G. and Boardman, J. D. (2017). Racial Disparities in Health Conditions among Prisoners Compared with the General Population. *SSM – Population Health*, 3, pp. 487–496.

O'Sullivan, J. (2015). White Officer Won't Face Charges in Shooting of 2 Black Men in Alleged Skateboard Assault in Olympia. *The Seattle Times*. [Online]. Available at: www.seattletimes.com/seat tle-news/cop-wont-face-charges-in-shooting-of-2-alleged-shop lifters-in-olympia-5 [Accessed Oct. 2023].

Office of Financial Management. (2011). Tribal Areas – 2010 Census Detailed Demographic Profile. Office of Finance Management. [Online]. Available at: https://ofm.wa.gov/washington-data-resea rch/population-demographics/decennial-census/census-2010/ 2010-census-detailed-demographic-profiles/tribal-areas-2010-census-detailed-demographic-profile [Accessed Oct. 2023].

Office of Justice Programs. (2022). *Drug Courts*. Washington, DC: U.S Department of Justice.

Ostrom, B. J., Hamblin, L. E. and Schauffler, R. Y. (2020). *Delivering Timely Justice in Criminal Cases: A National Picture*. Williamsburg, VA: National Center for State Courts.

Perry, D. M. and Carter-Long, L. (2016). The Ruderman White Paper on Media Coverage of Law Enforcement Use of Force and Disability: A Media Study (2013–2015) and Overview. Ruderman Family Foundation. [Online]. Available at: https://rudermanfou ndation.org/wp-content/uploads/2017/08/MediaStudy-PoliceD isability_final-final.pdf [Accessed Oct. 2023].

Pettinati, H. M., Belden, P. P., Evans, B. D., Ruetsch, C. R., Meyers, K. and Jensen, J. M. (1996). The Natural History of Outpatient Alcohol and Drug Abuse Treatment in a Private Healthcare Setting. *Alcohol: Clinical and Experimental Research*, 20(5), pp. 847–852.

Pew Charitable Trusts. (2022). *Drug Arrests Stayed High Even as Imprisonment Fell from 2009 to 2019*. Washington, DC: s.n.

Pfeffer, F. T. (2018). Growing Wealth Gaps in Education. *Demography,* 55(3), pp. 1033–1068.

Pierson, E., Simoiu, C., Overgoor, J. Corbett-Davies, S., Jenson, D., Shoemaker, A., Ramachandran, V., Barghouty, P., Phillips, C., Shroff, R. and Goel, S. (2020). A Large-Scale Analysis of Racial Disparities in Police Stops across the United States. *Nature Human Behaviour*, 4, pp. 736–745.

Radovsky, S. (2018). *Andre Thompson and Bryson Chaplin Explain How It Feels to Survive a Police Shooting.* s.l.: Teen Vogue.

Ramanathan, S., Balasubramanian, N. and Faraone, S. V. (2017). Familial Transient Financial Difficulties during Infancy and Long-Term Developmental Concerns. *Psychological Medicine*, 47(12), pp. 2197–2204.

Raphael, S. (2021). The Intended and Unintended Consequences of Ban the Box. *Annual Review of Criminology*, 4, pp. 191–207.

Reavis, J. A., Looman, J., Franco, K. A. and Rojas, B. (2013). Adverse Childhood Experiences and Adult Criminality: How Long Must We Live before We Possess Our Own Lives? *The Permanente Journal*, 17(2), pp. 44–48.

Reis, T. (2022). Trayvon Martin's Death Set Off a Movement That Shaped a Decade's Defining Moments. 25 February. *The Washington Post*. [Online]. Available at: www.washingtonpost.com/nation/2022/02/25/trayvon-martins-death-set-off-movement-that-shaped-decades-defining-moments/ [Accessed Oct. 2023].

Renville, F. (2011). The Shooting Death of John T. Williams. 21 February. *Indian Country Today*. [Online]. Available at: https://ictnews.org/archive/the-shooting-death-of-john-t-williams.

Roberts, M., Reither, E. N. and Lim, S. (2020). Contributors to the Black-White Life Expectancy Gap in Washington D.C. *Nature*, 10.

Rosoff, H. (2016). *Man Killed by Thurston Co. Deputy Identified.* Seattle, WA: KIRO 7.

Ross, C. T. (2015). A Multi-Level Bayesian Analysis of Racial Bias in Police Shootings at the County-Level in the United States, 2011–2014. *PLOS ONE*. https://doi.org/10.1371/journal.pone.0141854

Rossler, M. T. and Terrill, W. (2016). Mental Illness, Police Use of Force, and Citizen Injury. *Police Quarterly*, 20(2). https://doi.org/10.1177/1098611116681480

Savolainen, J. (2006). Inequality, Welfare State, and Homicide: Further Support for the Institutional Anomie Theory. *Criminology*. https://doi.org/10.1111/j.1745-9125.2000.tb01413.x

Schnepel, K. (2016). Good Jobs and Recidivism. *The Economic Journal*. https://doi.org/10.1111/ecoj.12415

Sered, D. (2019). *Until We Reckon*. New York: The New Press.

Shem-Tov, Y., Raphael, S. and Skog, A. (2022). Can Restorative Justice Conferencing Reduce Recidivism? Evidence from the Make-It-Right Program. *National Bureau of Economic Research*. [Online.] Available at: https://doi.org/10.3386/w29150

Shen, Y., Bushway, S. D., Sorensen, L. C. and Smith, H. L. (2020). Locking up My Generation: Cohort Differences in Prison Spells over the Life Course. *Criminology*, 6 July. pp. 1–33.

Siegel, M., Rieders, M., Rieders, H., Moumneh, J., Asfour, J., Oh, J. and Oh, S. (2022). Measuring Structural Racism and Its Association with Racial Disparities in Firearm Homicide. *Journal of Racial and Ethnic Health Disparities*, 12, pp. 1–16.

Singer, S. (2014). *America's Safest City: Delinquency and Modernity in Suburbia*. New York City: New York University Press.

Smart, C., Fischer, A. and Krolik, A. (2021). The Most Detailed Map of New York City Mayoral Primary Results. *The New York Times*. [Online]. Available at: www.nytimes.com/interactive/2021/06/23/nyregion/nyc-mayor-primary-results-precinct-map.html [Accessed Oct. 2023].

Swaner, R. (2022). 'We Can't Get No Nine-to-Five': New York City Gang Membership as a Response to the Structural Violence of Everyday Life. *Critical Criminology*, 30, pp. 95–111.

Sykes, C. L. and Maroto, M. (2016). A Wealth of Inequalities: Mass Incarceration, Employment, and Racial Disparities in U.S. Household Wealth, 1996 to 2011. *The Russell Sage Foundation Journal of the Social Sciences*, October, 2(6), pp. 129–152.

Tate, S. R., Mrnak-Meyer, J., Shriver, C. L., Atkinson, J. H., Robinson, S. K. and Brown, S. A. (2011). Predictors of Treatment Retention for Substance-Dependent Adults with Co-occurring Depression. *The American Journal on Addictions,* 20(4), pp. 357–365.

Team, I. E. (2021). FAQ: What is a Third-Party Background Check? [Online]. Available at: www.indeed.com/career-advice/starting-new-job/what-is-third-party-background-check [Accessed July 2022].

Thacher, D. (2004). The Rich Get Richer and the Poor Get Robbed: Inequality in US Criminal Victimization, 1974–2000. *Journal of Quantitative Criminology*, 20, pp. 89–116.

Thompson, A. and Tapp, N. T. (2022). *Criminal Victimization, 2021.* Washington, DC: Bureau of Justice Statistics.

UCI Newkirk Center for Science & Society, Michigan State University College of Law, University of Michigan: Michigan Law. (2023). *The National Registry of Exonerations.* s.l.: s.n. [Online]. Available at: www.law.umich.edu/special/exoneration/Pages/detaillist.aspx

Ulmer, J. T., Harris, C. T. and Steffensmeier, D. (2012). Racial and Ethnic Disparities in Structural Disadvantage and Crime: White, Black, and Hispanic Comparisons. *Social Science Quarterly*, 93(3), pp. 799–819.

United States Census Bureau. (2023). My Tribal Area. [Online]. Available at: www.census.gov/tribal/ [Accessed Aug. 2022].

United States Department of Labor, Wage and Hour Division (WHD). (2021). Fiscal Year Data for WHD. [Online]. Available at: www.dol.gov/agencies/whd/data/charts#panel1 [Accessed May 2023].

U.S. Department of Education. (2017). *Campus Safety and Security Survey, 2008–2016*. Washington, DC: s.n.

Velez, M. B., Krivo, L. J. and Peterson, R. D. (2003). Structural Inequality and Homicide: An Assessment of the Black-White Gap in Killings. *Criminology*, 41(3), pp. 645–672.

Vera Institute of Justice. (2023). Incarceration Trends. [Online]. Available at: https://github.com/vera-institute/incarceration-tre nds [Accessed Aug. 2022].

Weaver, V. M., Papachristos, A. and Zanger-Tishler, M. (2019). The Great Decoupling: The Disconnection between Criminal Offender and Experience of Arrest across Two Cohorts. *The Russell Sage Foundation Journal of the Social Sciences,* 5(1), pp. 89–123.

Wickham, S., Whitehead, M., Taylor-Robinson, D. and Barr, B. (2017). The Effect of a Transition into Poverty on a Child and Maternal Mental Health: A Longitudinal Analysis of the UK Millennium Cohort Study. *The Lancet*, March, pp. E141–E148.

Wilkinson, R. (2010). Why is Violence More Common Where Inequality is Greater? *Annals of the New York Academy of Sciences*, 23 July.

Wolff, N. and Shi, J. (2009). Contextualization of Physical and Sexual Assault in Male Prisons: Incidents and Their Aftermath. *Journal of Correctional Health Care*, 15(1), pp. 58–82.

Index

www.ingramcontent.com/pod-product-compliance
Lightning Source LLC
Chambersburg PA
CBHW070347270326
41926CB00017B/4026